PACEMAKER®

Basic
Mathematics

WORKBOOK

GLOBE FEARON
Pearson Learning Group

REVIEWERS
We thank the following educators, who provided valuable comments
and suggestions during the development of this book:

Rosemarie Estok, Woodbridge Public Schools, Woodbridge, New Jersey
Audris Griffith, Glen Bard West High School, Glen, Illinois
Dorie Knaub, Downey Unified School District, Downey, California
Christine Sweat, Highland Middle School, Jacksonville, Florida

Subject Area Consultant: Kay McClain, Department of Teaching and Learning,
Vanderbilt University, Nashville, Tennessee
Pacemaker Curriculum Advisor: Stephen C. Larsen, formerly of The University of Texas at Austin

Supervising Editor: Stephanie Petron Cahill
Senior Editor: Phyllis Dunsay
Editors: Dena Pollak, Bonnie Zitter
Writers: Cheryl E. Goldstein, Jennifer McCarthy
Production Editors: Laura Benford-Sullivan, Andrew Roney
Designers: Evelyn Bauer, Jennifer Visco
Photo Coordinator: Jennifer Hixson
Editorial Assistants: Kathy Bentzen, Wanda Rockwell
Market Manager: Donna Frasco
Research Director: Angela Darchi
Cover Design: Evelyn Bauer
Electronic Composition: Burmar Technical Corp., Linda Bierniak, Mimi Raihl, Phyllis Rosinsky

About the Cover: Mathematics is a way to help people understand and deal with their
environment. The images on the cover of this book show how an understanding of basic
mathematics is relevant in everyday life. Runners need to calculate their speed over distances.
Architects use geometric structures and formulas to build cities. Newspapers and magazines display
data visually in graphs. Mechanics use gearing ratios to repair machines such as cars and airplanes.
How do you use mathematics in your everyday life?

ISBN 0-835-93582-5
Printed in the United States of America
   7 8 9 10   04 05 03

1-800-321-3106
www.pearsonlearning.com

Contents

A Note to the Student

Use this workbook along with your *Pacemaker Basic Mathematics* textbook. Each exercise in the workbook is linked to a lesson in your textbook. This workbook will help you do three things—review, practice, and think critically.

Each exercise starts with a quick **review** to remind you of the basic math skills and concepts from the lesson. This boxed review shows you how to do the practice exercises that follow. You can also use this boxed review as a study tool. Use it whenever you want to review a skill. It will help you to remember what you've learned.

Practice in the skills and concepts of the lesson follow the boxed review. The more you practice, the more you will remember. Set goals for yourself, and try to meet them as you do each set of exercises. Practice helps you master skills and leads to success on tests, in school, at work, and in life.

Your **critical thinking** skills are challenged when you do the problems at the bottom of the page. Critical thinking—or to put it another way, thinking critically—means putting information to use. For example, you may review and practice how to multiply a cost by a percent. Then, you may have to use this information to find the discount and the new price of a CD on sale. That is, you will apply what you know to a different situation. This is critical thinking!

Your textbook is a wonderful source of knowledge. By studying it, you will learn a great deal about basic mathematics. But the real value of this information will come when you've mastered the basic math skills and put critical thinking to use.

Name _____ Date _____

1.1 What Is a Whole Number?   Exercise 1

Numbers get larger as you move to the right on the number line.

Write the missing numbers for each number line.

1.
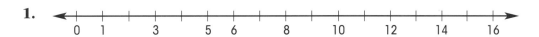

2.

3.

4.

5.

6.

7.

8.
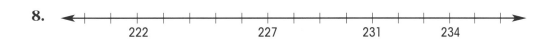

CRITICAL THINKING

On Interstate 80, there are markers for each mile. While Peter drove, Jan noticed markers for mile 203 then mile 204. She fell asleep for a few minutes. When she awoke, the first marker she saw was for mile 210. List the mile markers they passed while Jan was asleep.

▶ 1.2 Odd and Even Numbers   Exercise 2

Even numbers end in 0, 2, 4, 6, or 8.   48 and 50 are even numbers.

Odd numbers end in 1, 3, 5, 7, and 9.   31 and 85 are odd numbers.

Circle the even numbers below.

1. 0 1 2 3 4 5

2. 15 16 17 18 19 20

3. 26 27 28 29 30 31

4. 62 63 64 65 66 67

5. 87 88 89 90 91 92

6. 200 201 202 203 204 205

7. 386 387 388 389 390 391

8. 423 424 425 426 427 428

Circle the odd numbers below.

9. 512 513 514 515 516 517

10. 6 7 8 9 10 11

11. 123 124 125 126 127 128

12. 456 457 458 459 460 461

13. 726 727 728 729 730 731

14. 958 959 960 961 962 963

15. 50 51 52 53 54 55 56

16. 814 815 816 817 818 819

CRITICAL THINKING

One ninth-grade class at Madison School has 15 girls and 14 boys.

1. Are there an even number of girls?
Why or why not?

2. During a fire drill, students must leave
the building in pairs. Will each ninth-grade
student have a partner? Why or why not?

Name _____ Date _____

Rename each number to show the place value of each digit.

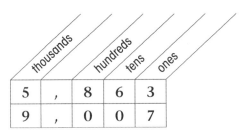

5,863 means **5 thousands + 8 hundreds + 6 tens + 3 ones**

9,007 means **9 thousands + 7 ones**

The place value of each digit in a number is shown below. Write the number.

1. 9 thousands + 5 tens + 6 ones   _____

2. 7 thousands + 1 hundred + 8 tens + 3 ones   _____

3. 8 thousands + 3 hundreds + 5 ones   _____

4. 2 thousands + 7 tens   _____

Rename each number to show the place value of each digit.

5. 8,954   _____

6. 7,080   _____

7. 7,200   _____

8. 3,105   _____

CRITICAL THINKING

What number comes before 5,000 on the number line?

Name _____   Date _____

▶ 1.4 Place Value to Millions   Exercise 4

Look at the place-value chart.
Find the value of the underlined digit.
        3<u>5</u>,904,082

Find the place value of the underlined digit in each number.

1. 5,2<u>3</u>4 _____   **2.** 7,<u>4</u>02 _____

3. <u>9</u>,200 _____   **4.** 1<u>2</u>3,456 _____

5. <u>6</u>82,407 _____   **6.** 50,<u>4</u>73 _____

7. <u>4</u>78,209 _____   **8.** 6<u>8</u>0,473 _____

9. <u>2</u>16,400 _____   **10.** 50<u>7</u>,412 _____

11. <u>5</u>,846,701 _____   **12.** 8<u>5</u>0,763,142 _____

13. 123,456,78<u>9</u> _____   **14.** 9<u>8</u>7,456,000 _____

CRITICAL THINKING

1. Why is $10,000,000 worth more than $100,000?

2. Why is $200,000 worth more than $20,000?

Name_____ Date_____

> ## 1.5 Reading and Writing Whole Numbers   Exercise 5

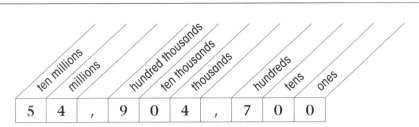

| 5 | 4 | , | 9 | 0 | 4 | , | 7 | 0 | 0 |

54 million, 904 thousand, 7 hundred
fifty-four million, nine hundred four thousand, seven hundred

Read each number. Write each number in words.

1. 368   _____

2. 87,934   _____

3. 124,587   _____

4. 8,206,059   _____

Use digits to write each number.

5. Twelve thousand, three hundred forty-five   _____

6. Fifty-three million, eighty-nine thousand, seven hundred two · _____

7. Two hundred fifty-six thousand, seven hundred eighty   _____

8. Eighty-five thousand, nine   _____

CRITICAL THINKING

It is two hundred thirty-eight thousand, eight hundred
fifty-seven miles from the Earth to the Moon. Write this
number using digits.

Name_____ Date_____

You can use symbols to show if a number is larger than, smaller than, or the same as another number.

$56 > 45$	$75 < 705$	$7 = 7$
56 **is greater than** 45.	75 **is less than** 705.	7 **is equal to** 7.

Compare each pair of numbers from left to right. Use the symbol >, <, or =.

1. 368 _____ 852   **2.** 24 _____ 57   **3.** 258 _____ 257

4. 1,203 _____ 1,208   **5.** 5,469 _____ 5,469   **6.** 6,874 _____ 6,247

7. 489 _____ 259   **8.** 356 _____ 356   **9.** 789 _____ 589

10. 56,987 _____ 56,957   **11.** 42,357 _____ 42,537   **12.** 357 _____ 357

13. 7,012 _____ 7,028   **14.** 62,508 _____ 62,708   **15.** 98,671 _____ 98,761

16. 78,650 _____ 78,650   **17.** 23,600 _____ 23,006   **18.** 8,520 _____ 8,250

CRITICAL THINKING

Solve each problem. Show your work.

1. There are two swimming pools in our neighborhood. One contains 51,712 gallons of water, and the other contains 52,580 gallons of water. Which pool is bigger?

2. John has to buy weed killer for his yard. He compares two different brands. Brand A makes 24 gallons of weed killer and Brand B makes 32 gallons. It takes 28 gallons to do the lawn. Which weed killer should he buy? Why?

▶ 1.7 Ordering Whole Numbers   Exercise 7

To order numbers, first count the digits and then compare.

smallest number → 864 ← 3 digits
5,790 ← 4 digits
5,470 ← 4 digits
↑
4 is less than 7

The numbers, from least to greatest are: 864   5,470   5,790.

Order the numbers from least to greatest.

1. 24	**2.** 152	**3.** 2,305	**4.** 698
17	178	705	1,258
45	165	505	742

5. 2,587	**6.** 65,874	**7.** 654,321	**8.** 968,548
951	45,128	423,159	254,129
1,247	187,542	147,258	540,068

9. 54,852   32,210   23,568   **10.** 98,000   85,001   79,012

11. 65,150   94,127   75,145   **12.** 64,236   54,147   85,147

CRITICAL THINKING

**Which set of numbers is in order from greatest to least?
Circle the correct answer.**

a. 7,070   7,707   7,007

b. 8,880   8,808   8,088

c. 6,611   6,116   6,161

1.8 Problem Solving: Reading Tables   Exercise 8

U.S. Magazines	
Magazine	**Subscriptions**
Consumers Digest	1,254,879
Motor Trend	968,719
Popular Science	1,805,525
Reader's Digest	15,103,830
Seventeen	2,172,923
TV Guide	13,175,549

Use the table above to answer the questions below.

1. Which magazine had the largest number of subscriptions? _____

2. Which magazine had the smallest number of subscriptions? _____

3. Did more people buy *TV Guide* or *Consumers Digest?* _____

4. If 10,000 more people bought *Motor Trend* magazine,
   what would be its number of subscriptions? _____

5. Make a table. List the magazines in order from the greatest
   to the least number of subscriptions.

6. Which of these magazines would you buy? _____
   Was this magazine in first place on the table
   you made for Question 5? Why or why not? _____

   _____

▶ 1.9 Rounding Whole Numbers   **Exercise 9**

Round the number 5,683 to the nearest hundred.

Underline the digit in the rounding place.	5,<u>6</u>83
Look at the digit to the right.	↑
Compare this digit to 5.	8 is greater than 5.
Since 8 is greater than 5,	5,<u>6</u>83
add 1 to the rounding place.	5 <u>7</u> → Add 1 to 6.
Change the digits to the right to 0.	5,700

5,683 rounded to the nearest hundred is 5,700.

Round each number to the nearest ten.

1. 214 _____   **2.** 357 _____   **3.** 965 _____

4. 5,684 _____   **5.** 9,571 _____   **6.** 65,924 _____

Round each number to the nearest hundred.

7. 689 _____   **8.** 253 _____   **9.** 147 _____

10. 68,594 _____   **11.** 71,852 _____   **12.** 349,574 _____

Round each number to the nearest thousand.

13. 6,325 _____   **14.** 2,587 _____   **15.** 97,451 _____

16. 59,845 _____   **17.** 852,741 _____   **18.** 396,399 _____

CRITICAL THINKING

What three numbers might round to 600?

2.1 What Is Addition?   Exercise 10

Addition problems may be written in both horizontal form and vertical form.

Horizontal form	Vertical form
$8 + 4 = 12$	$\begin{array}{r} 8 \\ + \ 4 \\ \hline 12 \end{array}$

Write each addition problem in horizontal form using numbers.

1. Four plus three equals seven. _____

2. Six plus five equals eleven. _____

3. Eight plus zero equals eight. _____

4. Three plus seven equals ten. _____

Write each addition problem in vertical form using numbers.

5. $4 + 6 = 10$ **6.** $8 + 7 = 15$ **7.** $0 + 14 = 14$

8. $5 + 7 = 12$ **9.** $2 + 5 = 7$ **10.** $8 + 3 = 11$

CRITICAL THINKING

Write each addition problem in horizontal form using numbers.

1. The school bus stops 4 times on Roscoe Street. It stops 3 times on Elm Street. The bus stops 7 times on the two streets.

2. There were 2 students on the school bus. The bus stopped to pick up 3 more students. There are now 5 students on the bus.

_____   _____

Name_____ Date_____

The number line shows that $4 + 5 = 9$.

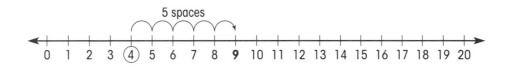

Use a number line to add.

1. 6
      + 5

2. 7
      + 3

3. 8
      + 4

4. 2
      + 4

5. 5
      + 5

6. 7
      + 6

7. 0
      + 8

8. 5
      + 4

9. 9
      + 8

10. 7
       + 7

11. 8
       + 7

12. 6
       + 9

13. $6 + 0 =$

14. $8 + 8 =$

15. $2 + 8 =$

16. $5 + 8 =$

17. $6 + 7 =$

18. $9 + 0 =$

19. $8 + 3 =$

20. $5 + 7 =$

CRITICAL THINKING

Write the addition problem for each number line shown below.

1.

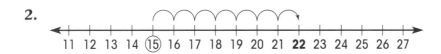

2.

▶ 2.3 Column Addition   Exercise 12

Remember to write the numbers in a column.

Add. $3 + 6 + 2 + 5$

```
 3 ⎤
   ⎬9
 6 ⎦   ⎤
        ⎬16
 2 ⎤   ⎦
   ⎬7
+5 ⎦
────
 16
```

1.   3   **2.**   2   **3.**   4   **4.**   7
          8   9   5   8
        + 2   + 5   + 6   + 2
        ───   ───   ───   ───

5.   3   **6.**   9   **7.**   7   **8.**   8
          4   6   3   6
        + 2   + 1   + 4   + 3
        ───   ───   ───   ───

9.   6   **10.**   6   **11.**   5   **12.**   8
          9   7   6   3
        + 0   + 3   + 4   + 7
        ───   ───   ───   ───

13. $7 + 8 + 4 + 2 =$ **14.** $2 + 7 + 3 + 4 =$ **15.** $2 + 6 + 0 + 3 =$

16. $0 + 7 + 4 + 8 =$ **17.** $3 + 9 + 4 + 1 =$ **18.** $6 + 8 + 2 + 4 =$

CRITICAL THINKING

The odd numbers 1, 3, 5, 7, and 9 are missing from this square. Fill in the missing numbers. The sum in each row and each column should be 15.

2		6
4		8

▶ 2.4 Adding Larger Numbers   Exercise 13

Remember to line up the digits in each number by place value.

Add.   6,542 + 236

```
   6,542
 +   236
   6,778
```

Add.

| **1.** | 7,034
+   624 | **2.** | 8,674
+ 1,225 | **3.** | 4,321
+ 5,243 | **4.** | 9,347
+   122 |

| **5.** | 4,372
+ 1,507 | **6.** | 2,138
+ 3,621 | **7.** | 7,005
+   944 | **8.** | 8,123
+ 1,765 |

9. 5,987 + 6,012 =   **10.** 6,258 + 431 =

11. 7,813 + 1,176 =   **12.** 5,467 + 4,532 =

13. 9,676 + 3,321 =   **14.** 1,234 + 5,621 =

CRITICAL THINKING

Are the following sums odd or even numbers?

1. The sum of two even numbers is _____.

2. The sum of two odd numbers is _____.

3. The sum of an odd number and an even number is _____.

2.5 Problem Solving: Clue Words for Addition

These clue words tell you to add.

in all   *together*   *altogether*   *total*   *both*

READ the problem. Look for clue words. Make a PLAN. DO the plan to solve the problem.

1. Jason and Tim went to the local department store. Jason purchased a new television set for $137. Tim purchased a new video game for $60. How much did both Jason and Tim spend?

2. Alice and José went shopping together. Alice spent $43. José spent $56. How much did they spend in all?

3. A cafeteria served 51 women, 45 men, and 23 children in one day. On that day, how many people did the cafeteria serve altogether?

4. During the video game, Brea scored 176 points. Sean scored 220 points. Together, how many points did they score?

5. Lori played a game. She scored 131 points on her first turn. She scored 58 points on her second turn. What was her total score?

6. There are 217 men and 232 women working at Woodson Electronics. How many people work there altogether?

2.6 Adding with One Regrouping   Exercise 15

Remember to regroup when the sum is 10 or greater.

Add.   124 + 649

$$
\begin{array}{r}
{}^{1} \\
124 \\
+\ 649 \\
\hline
773
\end{array}
$$

Add.

1.   38
       + 4

2.   52
       + 9

3.   37
       + 54

4.   67
       + 25

5.   77
       + 16

6.   323
       + 168

7.   543
       + 239

8.   627
       + 224

9. 566 + 428 =

10. 829 + 154 =

11. 258 + 671 =

12. 648 + 203 =

13. 754 + 92 =

14. 82 + 865 =

CRITICAL THINKING

Find the error in each problem below. Then correct the problem.

1.   7,903
       + 506
       _____
        12,963

2.   457
       + 506
       _____
        953

3.   400
       + 551
       _____
        901

Name _____   Date _____

2.7 Adding with More Than One Regrouping

Sometimes when you add numbers, you need to regroup more than once.

Add.   2,986 + 1,304

$$
\begin{array}{r}
{}^{1}\ {}^{1} \\
2,986 \\
+\ 1,304 \\
\hline
4,290
\end{array}
$$

Add. Do not forget to regroup.

1. 2,042 + 3,985	**2.** 6,902 + 3,088	**3.** 5,581 + 3,819	**4.** 2,147 + 7,948
5. 2,598 + 6,075	**6.** 5,432 + 7,881	**7.** 3,568 + 8,548	**8.** 6,951 + 7,513

9. 4,581 + 6,872 =   **10.** 2,384 + 459 =

11. 4,567 + 9,876 =   **12.** 235 + 951 + 4,587 =

13. 654 + 987 + 1,230 =   **14.** 8,520 + 7,410 + 3,069 =

CRITICAL THINKING

Solve each problem. Show your work.

1. Boston is 1,933 kilometers from St. Louis.
   St. Louis is 3,414 kilometers from San Francisco.
   How far is it from Boston to San Francisco if you
   go through St. Louis?

2. New York is 557 miles from Columbus, Ohio.
   Columbus is 2,266 miles from Los Angeles.
   How far is it from New York to Los Angeles if
   you go through Columbus?

▶ 2.8 Estimating Sums   Exercise 17

Use rounding to estimate 549 + 321 + 89.

Round each number to the nearest hundred.   549 →   500 Add the
                                                        321 →   300 rounded
                                                         89 → + 100 numbers.
                                                              900

Estimate each sum to the nearest hundred.

1.	562	2.	950	3.	605	4.	582
	+ 184		+ 810		+ 184		+ 426

5.	824	6.	195	7.	653	8.	982
	+ 952		+ 286		+ 238		+ 237

Use estimation to check each exact sum. If an answer does not make sense, find the correct sum.

9.	482	10.	504	11.	669	12.	229
	92		23		789		479
	+ 620		+ 782		+ 403		+ 43
	1,194		1,109		1,561		751

13.	981	14.	672	15.	123	16.	142
	23		830		475		672
	+ 80		+ 407		+ 303		+ 932
	1,084		2,109		1,901		1,746

CRITICAL THINKING

At one time, the population of Illinois was 11,430,602.

1. What is this population rounded to the nearest million?

2. What is this population rounded to the nearest ten million?

▶ 3.1 What Is Subtraction?   Exercise 18

> Subtraction problems may be written in both horizontal and vertical form.
>
> Horizontal form   Vertical form
> $9 - 5 = 4$
> $$\begin{array}{r} 9 \\ -\ 5 \\ \hline 4 \end{array}$$
>
> Remember that order in subtraction is important.

Write each subtraction problem in horizontal form using numbers.

1. Eighteen minus ten equals eight.   _____

2. Seven minus seven equals zero.   _____

3. Thirteen minus six equals seven.   _____

4. Six minus zero equals six.   _____

Write each subtraction problem in vertical form using numbers.

5. $10 - 4 = 6$ **6.** $14 - 9 = 5$ **7.** $6 - 3 = 3$

8. $18 - 0 = 18$ **9.** $12 - 5 = 7$ **10.** $15 - 7 = 8$

CRITICAL THINKING

Write the subtraction problem in horizontal form using numbers.

Judy had ten pencils. She gave seven
away to Ann. Judy now has three pencils. _____

▶ 3.2 Basic Subtraction   Exercise 19

The number line shows that $16 - 9 = 7$.

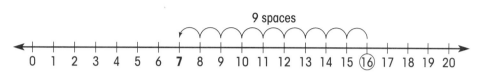

9 spaces

0 1 2 3 4 5 6 **7** 8 9 10 11 12 13 14 15 ⑯ 17 18 19 20

Use a number line to subtract.

1. 8 − 3	**2.** 13 − 5	**3.** 16 − 9	**4.** 10 − 4

5. 15 − 6	**6.** 9 − 3	**7.** 13 − 7	**8.** 17 − 8

9. 12 − 6	**10.** 11 − 3	**11.** 16 − 8	**12.** 10 − 10

13. $14 - 6 =$ **14.** $15 - 7 =$ **15.** $12 - 9 =$ **16.** $16 - 3 =$

17. $13 - 8 =$ **18.** $11 - 0 =$ **19.** $17 - 3 =$ **20.** $12 - 7 =$

CRITICAL THINKING

Find the missing numbers.

1.   14
− ■
―――
   5
	2. 19
	− ■
	―――
	   0
		3. 16
		− ■
		―――
		  16
			4. 7
			− ■
			―――
			   5

3.3 Subtracting Larger Numbers   Exercise 20

Remember to line up the digits in each number by place value.

Subtract.   6,578 − 436

$$\begin{array}{r} 6,578 \\ -436 \\ \hline 6,142 \end{array}$$

Subtract.

1. $\begin{array}{r} 43 \\ -31 \\ \hline \end{array}$
2. $\begin{array}{r} 79 \\ -52 \\ \hline \end{array}$
3. $\begin{array}{r} 77 \\ -23 \\ \hline \end{array}$
4. $\begin{array}{r} 86 \\ -42 \\ \hline \end{array}$

5. $\begin{array}{r} 182 \\ -62 \\ \hline \end{array}$
6. $\begin{array}{r} 456 \\ -234 \\ \hline \end{array}$
7. $\begin{array}{r} 9,872 \\ -6,310 \\ \hline \end{array}$
8. $\begin{array}{r} 4,798 \\ -32 \\ \hline \end{array}$

9. 478 − 343 =

10. 508 − 205 =

11. 492 − 81 =

12. 999 − 63 =

13. 789 − 67 =

14. 598 − 36 =

CRITICAL THINKING

Michael had two problems wrong on his subtraction quiz.
Find the incorrect problems and correct them.

1. $\begin{array}{r} 583 \\ -62 \\ \hline 521 \end{array}$
2. $\begin{array}{r} 789 \\ -64 \\ \hline 149 \end{array}$
3. $\begin{array}{r} 4,249 \\ -1,032 \\ \hline 3,216 \end{array}$
4. $\begin{array}{r} 5,826 \\ -1,314 \\ \hline 4,512 \end{array}$

3.4 Problem Solving: Clue Words for Subtraction

Exercise 21

> These clue words tell you to subtract.
>
> | how much more | left |
> | how much less | remain |
> | how many more | difference |

READ the problem. Look for clue words. Make a PLAN. DO the plan to solve the problem.

1. In September, Jack had 4,000 pieces of notebook paper. By June, he had used up 3,000 pieces of paper. How many pieces of paper are left?

2. Samantha has $44.50. Tawayka has $55.75. How much more money does Tawayka have than Samantha?

3. There are 3,780 books in the library. If 670 students borrow one book each from the library, how many books will remain?

4. Bianca drove 55 miles on Monday. She drove 96 miles on Tuesday. How many more miles did she drive on Tuesday than on Monday?

5. Kevin read 8 books in October. He read 12 books in November. How many more books did he read in November than in October?

6. Dwayne bought a radio for $96. Julia bought one for $88. How much more did Dwayne pay for the radio than Julia?

▶ 3.5 Subtracting with One Regrouping   Exercise 22

Remember to regroup when the bottom number is larger than the top number.

Subtract. 2,670 − 349

$$
\begin{array}{r}
\overset{610}{2,6\cancel{7}\cancel{0}} \\
-\ \ \ 349 \\
\hline
2,321
\end{array}
$$

Subtract. Remember to regroup. Show your work.

1.   65
    − 46

2.   731
    − 618

3.   1,456
    − 932

4.   52
    − 9

5.   926
    − 835

6.   84
    − 76

7.   387
    − 96

8.   2,627
    − 446

9. 4,568 − 3,449 =

10. 7,987 − 4,895 =

11. 3,456 − 531 =

12. 2,990 − 1,965 =

13. 6,351 − 1,045 =

14. 5,243 − 4,128 =

CRITICAL THINKING

Solve the following problem. Show your work.

Katrina had $46. Her friend borrowed $37. How much money does she have left?

▶ 3.6 Subtracting with More Than One Regrouping

Sometimes when you subtract numbers, you need to regroup more than once.

Subtract.   645 − 447

$$
\begin{array}{r}
\overset{\scriptscriptstyle 13}{} \\
\overset{\scriptscriptstyle 5\,\cancel{3}\,15}{\cancel{645}} \\
-\ 447 \\
\hline
198
\end{array}
$$

Subtract. Remember to regroup. Show your work.

1. $\begin{array}{r} 134 \\ -\ 35 \\ \hline \end{array}$

2. $\begin{array}{r} 578 \\ -\ 489 \\ \hline \end{array}$

3. $\begin{array}{r} 361 \\ -\ 169 \\ \hline \end{array}$

4. $\begin{array}{r} 7,671 \\ -\ 790 \\ \hline \end{array}$

5. $\begin{array}{r} 673 \\ -\ 74 \\ \hline \end{array}$

6. $\begin{array}{r} 2,124 \\ -\ 1,433 \\ \hline \end{array}$

7. $\begin{array}{r} 7,254 \\ -\ 6,165 \\ \hline \end{array}$

8. $\begin{array}{r} 461 \\ -\ 285 \\ \hline \end{array}$

9. 3,546 − 77 =

10. 5,786 − 5,699 =

11. 9,254 − 76 =

12. 584 − 188 =

13. 8,230 − 42 =

14. 698 − 599 =

CRITICAL THINKING

Solve each problem. Show your work.

1. Jamie received $1,120 in her paycheck. She owes $366 for her car payment. How much of her paycheck will remain after she pays her car payment?

2. Sid had $300. He bought a pair of boots for $99. How much money does he have left?

Name _____ Date _____

▶ **3.7 Regrouping with Zeros**   **Exercise 24**

When you subtract from zero, you need to regroup.

Subtract.   700 − 156

$$
\begin{array}{r}
{\scriptstyle 6\,9\,10}\\
\cancel{700}\\
-\ 156\\
\hline
544
\end{array}
$$

Subtract. Remember to regroup for ones, tens, and hundreds as needed.

1. 400
    − 67

2. 4,004
    − 2,773

3. 50,050
    − 21,653

4. 30,032
    −   71

5. 80,800
    − 42,991

6. 3,000
    − 722

7. 45,000
    − 7,679

8. 89,010
    − 55,827

9. 72,200 − 51,374 =

10. 70,220 − 46,211 =

11. 401 − 32 =

12. 900 − 9 =

13. 45,098 − 8,743 =

14. 73,062 − 64,901 =

CRITICAL THINKING
Solve each problem. Show your work.

1. Danny spent $100 for a sweater and a pair of jeans. The sweater cost $46. How much did the jeans cost?

2. Ana read 440 pages in her book. Her book has a total of 1,000 pages. How many more pages does Ana have to read?

▶ 3.8 Problem Solving: Add or Subtract?   Exercise 25

The following clue words will help you decide when to add or subtract.

Addition			Subtraction	
altogether	*total*	*in all*	*remain*	*difference*

READ the problem. Look for clue words. Make a PLAN.
DO the plan to solve the problem.

1. Zack bought a pair of jeans for $39, a shirt for $25, and a sweater for $50. What is the total cost of the three items?

2. Sami bought a box of pens for $2 and a notebook for $10. What was the difference in the two prices?

3. Rodrigo saved $350 last week and $467 this week. How much money did he save altogether?

4. The lead actor in the school play has to memorize 600 lines. He has only memorized 475. How many lines remain to be memorized?

5. Josie drove 1,500 miles in 3 days. She drove 400 miles on Tuesday and 350 miles on Wednesday. In all, how many miles did she drive on Monday and Tuesday?

6. Terrell saved $270 the first week, $145 the second week, and $450 the third week. How much more money did he save during the third week than during the first week?

▶ 4.1 What Is Multiplication   Exercise 26

The addition problem $2 + 2 + 2 + 2 + 2 + 2 = 12$ can be written as a multiplication problem in horizontal form or vertical form.

Horizontal form   Vertical form
$6 \times 2 = 12$ $\begin{array}{r} 6 \\ \times\ 2 \\ \hline 12 \end{array}$

Write each addition problem as a multiplication problem in horizontal form.

1. $1 + 1 + 1 + 1 = 4$ _____   **2.** $7 + 7 + 7 + 7 + 7 = 35$ _____

3. $5 + 5 = 10$ _____   **4.** $3 + 3 + 3 + 3 + 3 + 3 = 18$ _____

Write each multiplication problem in vertical form.

5. $9 \times 7 = 63$ **6.** $5 \times 4 = 20$ **7.** $8 \times 8 = 64$

8. $6 \times 5 = 30$ **9.** $6 \times 9 = 54$ **10.** $8 \times 4 = 32$

CRITICAL THINKING

Write each multiplication problem as an addition problem.

1. $0 \times 2 = 0$ **2.** $1 \times 6 = 6$

Name _____ Date _____

▶ 4.2 Basic Multiplication   Exercise 27

You can use the multiplication table below to find 3×8.

Factor 8

x	0	1	2	3	4	5	6	7	8	9
0	0	0	0	0	0	0	0	0	0	0
1	0	1	2	3	4	5	6	7	8	9
2	0	2	4	6	8	10	12	14	16	18
3	0	3	6	9	12	15	18	21	24	27
4	0	4	8	12	16	20	24	28	32	36
5	0	5	10	15	20	25	30	35	40	45
6	0	6	12	18	24	30	36	42	48	54
7	0	7	14	21	28	35	42	49	56	63
8	0	8	16	24	32	40	48	56	64	72
9	0	9	18	27	36	45	54	63	72	81

Factor 3 → 3

Product
$3 \times 8 = 24$

Use the multiplication table to multiply.

1. $1 \times 9 =$ **2.** $3 \times 9 =$ **3.** $6 \times 6 =$ **4.** $8 \times 2 =$

5. $4 \times 8 =$ **6.** $4 \times 1 =$ **7.** $5 \times 9 =$ **8.** $5 \times 5 =$

9. $8 \times 3 =$ **10.** $7 \times 5 =$ **11.** $2 \times 2 =$ **12.** $1 \times 7 =$

13. $5 \times 2 =$ **14.** $2 \times 5 =$ **15.** $6 \times 8 =$ **16.** $8 \times 6 =$

CRITICAL THINKING

How many times does the number 24 appear in the multiplication table? Why does it appear more than once?

4.3 Multiplying Larger Numbers   Exercise 28

When you multiply larger numbers, multiply each place.

Multiply. 531×321

$$
\begin{array}{r}
531 \\
\times\ 321 \\
\hline
531 \\
10\ 620 \\
+\ 159\ 300 \\
\hline
170{,}451
\end{array}
$$

10 620   Write a zero in the **ones** place.

+ 159 300   Write zeros in the **tens** place and the **ones** place.

Multiply.

1.   61
       $\times\ 3$

2.   52
       $\times\ 4$

3.   94
       $\times\ 2$

4.   232
       $\times\ 3$

5.   24
       $\times\ 12$

6.   51
       $\times\ 15$

7.   93
       $\times\ 33$

8.   756
       $\times\ 11$

9. $921 \times 314 =$

10. $631 \times 321 =$

CRITICAL THINKING

Match each multiplication problem with its product.

1. 723
    $\times\ 1$

2. 723
    $\times\ 10$

3. 723
    $\times\ 100$

a. 72,300

b.   723

c. 7,230

Name _____ Date _____

▶ 4.4 Multiplying with One Regrouping   Exercise 29

Remember to regroup if you need to.

Multiply. 56×14

$$
\begin{array}{r}
\overset{2}{5}6 \\
\times\,14 \\
\hline
224 \\
+\,560 \\
\hline
784
\end{array}
$$
← Write a zero in the **ones** place.

Multiply. Regroup if you need to.

1. 436
     $\times\,5$

2. 517
     $\times\,4$

3. 629
     $\times\,8$

4. 278
     $\times\,2$

5.   28
     $\times\,17$

6.   54
     $\times\,25$

7.   73
     $\times\,34$

8.   84
     $\times\,12$

9. $712 \times 153 =$

10. $327 \times 118 =$

CRITICAL THINKING

Find the missing number in each multiplication problem.

1.   72
     $\times\,\blacksquare$
     288

2. $\overset{2}{4}8$
     $\times\,\blacksquare$
     144

3. $\overset{1\,2}{5}24$
     $\times\,\blacksquare$
     2,620

4.5 Multiplying with More Than One Regrouping

Remember that sometimes there will be more than one row of regrouping digits.

Multiply. 276×48

$$
\begin{array}{r}
\overset{32}{\cancel{64}} \\
276 \\
\times\ 48 \\
\hline
2208 \\
+\ 11040 \\
\hline
13{,}248
\end{array}
$$

Multiply.

1. $\begin{array}{r} 35 \\ \times\ 72 \\ \end{array}$
    2. $\begin{array}{r} 17 \\ \times\ 86 \\ \end{array}$
    3. $\begin{array}{r} 68 \\ \times\ 32 \\ \end{array}$
    4. $\begin{array}{r} 45 \\ \times\ 59 \\ \end{array}$

5. $\begin{array}{r} 235 \\ \times\ 42 \\ \end{array}$
    6. $\begin{array}{r} 174 \\ \times\ 36 \\ \end{array}$
    7. $\begin{array}{r} 482 \\ \times\ 39 \\ \end{array}$
    8. $\begin{array}{r} 546 \\ \times\ 51 \\ \end{array}$

9. $653 \times 157 =$
    10. $837 \times 265 =$

CRITICAL THINKING

Match each multiplication problem to its product without multiplying. Explain your thinking.

1. $\begin{array}{r} 671 \\ \times\ 3 \\ \end{array}$
    2. $\begin{array}{r} 671 \\ \times\ 25 \\ \end{array}$
    3. $\begin{array}{r} 671 \\ \times\ 427 \\ \end{array}$
    a. 16,775
b. 286,517
c. 2,013

Name _____ Date _____

4.6 Problem Solving: Clue Words for Multiplication   Exercise 31

These clue words tell you to multiply.

of   *for* 8 hours   *in* 12 months   *at* $95 each

READ the problem. Look for clue words. Make a PLAN. DO the plan to solve the problem.

1. The members of the drama club need 5 large boards for scenery. Each board costs $35. How much money do they need for all 5 boards?

2. Jasmine volunteered at the book fair to work for 8 hours. In 1 hour, she filled five shelves. How many shelves did she fill in 8 hours if she continued to work at that pace?

3. Lee ran 26 miles at a rate of 8 minutes per mile. For how many minutes did Lee run?

4. Red's Cineplex has seven movie theaters. Each theater can hold 535 people. On Saturday night, all the theaters were sold out for the 9:00 P.M. show. How many people saw movies at Red's Cineplex at 9:00 P.M. that night?

5. Ronnie works 36 hours per month. How many hours does he work in 12 months?

6. A school needs to buy 16 new hurdles for its track team. Each hurdle costs $55. How much will the 16 hurdles cost the school?

Name_____ Date_____

4.7 Multiplying Whole Numbers by 10, 100, 1,000

Remember to count the number of zeros when you multiply by 10, 100, or 1,000.

Multiply.

$645 \times 10 = 6,450$ $645 \times 100 = 64,500$ $645 \times 1,000 = 645,000$

    ↑   ↑   ↑   ↑   ↑   ↑

1 zero 1 zero   2 zeros 2 zeros   3 zeros 3 zeros

Multiply.

1. $7 \times 10 =$

2. $14 \times 10 =$

3. $10 \times 6 =$

4. $23 \times 100 =$

5. $824 \times 10 =$

6. $50 \times 100 =$

7. $3 \times 1,000 =$

8. $41,249 \times 100 =$

9. $420 \times 100 =$

10. $302 \times 1,000 =$

CRITICAL THINKING

Find the missing number in each multiplication problem.
Tell how you found each missing number.

1. $4 \times \underline{\hspace{1cm}} = 400$ **2.** $18 \times \underline{\hspace{1cm}} = 18,000$ **3.** $20 \times \underline{\hspace{1cm}} = 200$

4. $472 \times \underline{\hspace{1cm}} = 47,200$ **5.** $470 \times \underline{\hspace{1cm}} = 47,000$ **6.** $10 \times \underline{\hspace{1cm}} = 180$

bers That Contain Zero   Exercise 33

ltiply by zero the partial product is zero.

$$
\begin{array}{r}
\overset{\overset{1}{\cancel{3}}}{2}15 \\
\times\ 306 \\
\hline
1290 \\
0000 \leftarrow 215 \times 0 = 0 \\
+\ 64500 \\
\hline
65{,}790
\end{array}
$$

3.   470
        $\times$ 30

4.   46
        $\times$ 50

7.   304
        $\times$ 706

8.   460
        $\times$ 203

10. $418 \times 309 =$

$418 \times 301 =$ **3.** $418 \times 302 =$

$00) + (418 \times 2)?$

Name _____ Date _____

> Remember to answer the hidden question first.
>
> Elwood bought 8 fish for $3 each and a tank for $75. How much did h
> spend in all?
>
> **PLAN**   Multiply to find the cost of the fish.
>   Add to find how much he spent in all.
>
> **DO**   8 × $3 = $24   ← Cost of fish
> $24 + $75 = $99   ← Total cost
>
> The total cost is $99.

**READ the problem. Make a PLAN. DO the plan to solve
the problem.**

1. It took Bret 8 hours to get from his house to Washington,
   D.C. He drove at 55 miles per hour. He stopped for 2 hours
   along the way. How many miles did he drive?

2. Sharon is paid $5 an hour for the first 20 hours she works
   each week. For each extra hour, Sharon is paid $7. How
   much will Sharon earn if she works 28 hours this week?

3. Sergio wants to buy a coffee mug for each of his six teachers.
   A mug costs $4. Sergio pays with two $20 bills. How
   much change will he receive?

4. The owner of a restaurant gave 15 scholarships of $1,000
   each. She also donated $25,000 to the local high school.
   How much did she donate altogether?

5. Toby, Bea, and Miriam share expenses for their apartment.
   They each pay $300 a month for rent. Their gas and electric
   bill is $150 a month. How much does the apartment cost
   them each month? Each year?

5.1 What Is Division?   Exercise 35

Division problems may be written in two ways.

$12 \div 6 = 2$ $6\overline{)12}$ with quotient 2

Write each division problem two ways using numbers.

1. Twenty divided by five equals four.   _____

2. Thirty divided by five equals six.   _____

3. Twelve divided by three equals four.   _____

4. Eighteen divided by three equals six.   _____

Write each division problem another way using numbers.

5. $18 \div 6 = 3$ _____   6. $24 \div 6 = 4$ _____

7. $27 \div 9 = 3$ _____   8. $32 \div 8 = 4$ _____

9. $21 \div 7 = 3$ _____   10. $36 \div 4 = 9$ _____

CRITICAL THINKING

Circle the boxes below to show the groups in each division problem.

1. $15 \div 3 = 5$ □□□□□□□□□□□□□□□

2. $15 \div 5 = 3$ □□□□□□□□□□□□□□□

5.2 Basic Division

You can use the multiplication table below to find $36 \div 9$.

Quotient $36 \div 9 = 4$

x	0	1	2	3	4	5	6	7	8	9
0	0	0	0	0	0	0	0	0	0	0
1	0	1	2	3	4	5	6	7	8	9
2	0	2	4	6	8	10	12	14	16	18
3	0	3	6	9	12	15	18	21	24	27
4	0	4	8	12	16	20	24	28	32	36
5	0	5	10	15	20	25	30	35	40	45
6	0	6	12	18	24	30	36	42	48	54
7	0	7	14	21	28	35	42	49	56	63
8	0	8	16	24	32	40	48	56	64	72
9	0	9	18	27	36	45	54	63	72	81

Divisor 9

Dividend 36

Use the multiplication table to find each quotient.

1. $20 \div 4 =$ **2.** $32 \div 4 =$ **3.** $16 \div 4 =$ **4.** $10 \div 5 =$

5. $15 \div 3 =$ **6.** $14 \div 7 =$ **7.** $12 \div 3 =$ **8.** $24 \div 6 =$

9. $32 \div 8 =$ **10.** $28 \div 4 =$ **11.** $18 \div 2 =$ **12.** $8 \div 4 =$

13. $6\overline{)18}$ **14.** $2\overline{)12}$ **15.** $8\overline{)16}$ **16.** $6\overline{)36}$

17. $9\overline{)72}$ **18.** $8\overline{)64}$ **19.** $7\overline{)42}$ **20.** $7\overline{)56}$

CRITICAL THINKING

Solve.

James made $72 for 9 hours of work. What does he make per hour?

▶ 5.3 Dividing with Remainders   **Exercise 37**

The remainder is the number left over after dividing.

Divide.   11 ÷ 3

$$\begin{array}{r} 3\ R2 \\ 3\overline{)11} \\ -9 \\ \hline 2 \end{array}$$ ← Remainder

Divide. Remember to write the quotient above the ones place in 1-8.

1. $5\overline{)33}$ **2.** $4\overline{)26}$ **3.** $6\overline{)45}$ **4.** $3\overline{)17}$

5. $4\overline{)17}$ **6.** $7\overline{)46}$ **7.** $7\overline{)34}$ **8.** $8\overline{)59}$

9. 38 ÷ 6 =   **10.** 75 ÷ 9 =   **11.** 38 ÷ 4 =   **12.** 57 ÷ 8 =

13. 48 ÷ 9 =   **14.** 18 ÷ 4 =   **15.** 37 ÷ 7 =   **16.** 45 ÷ 7 =

CRITICAL THINKING

Solve. Show your work.

1. Chess is a game played by 2 people. There were 37 people who wanted to play in the chess tournament. How many games could be played at once? How many people could not play?

2. John wanted to pack 70 pounds of potatoes in 8-pound sacks. How many sacks of potatoes did John pack? How many pounds were left over?

▶ 5.4 Dividing Larger Numbers

Exercise 38

Decide where to place the first digit in the quotient.

Divide. $149 \div 8$

$$
\begin{array}{r}
18 \text{ R5} \\
8\overline{)149} \\
-8 \\
\hline
69 \\
-64 \\
\hline
5
\end{array}
$$

Divide. Some problems will have a remainder.

1. $4\overline{)96}$ **2.** $6\overline{)75}$ **3.** $5\overline{)95}$ **4.** $3\overline{)76}$

5. $7\overline{)248}$ **6.** $2\overline{)352}$ **7.** $4\overline{)524}$ **8.** $6\overline{)137}$

9. $5\overline{)367}$ **10.** $3\overline{)551}$ **11.** $4\overline{)652}$ **12.** $7\overline{)123}$

CRITICAL THINKING

Solve. Show your work.

1. Gerome had $345 worth of $5 bills. How many $5 bills did he have?

2. Nancy had 258 pounds of potting soil. She bagged it using 5-pound bags. How many bags did she fill? How many pounds of potting soil was left over?

5.5 Checking Division

Check the division problem.

$$\begin{array}{r} 18\ \text{R}5 \\ 8\overline{)149} \end{array} \rightarrow \begin{array}{r} 18 \\ \times\ 8 \\ \hline 144 \\ +\ 5 \\ \hline 149\ \checkmark \end{array}$$ ← The division is correct.

Check each answer. If the answer is incorrect, show the correct division.

1. $\dfrac{24}{4\overline{)96}}$

2. $\dfrac{162}{4\overline{)652}}$

3. $\dfrac{76\ \text{R}2}{5\overline{)382}}$

4. $\dfrac{180\ \text{R}1}{3\overline{)721}}$

Divide. Check each answer.

5. $2\overline{)489}$

6. $6\overline{)127}$

7. $4\overline{)259}$

8. $5\overline{)360}$

9. $3\overline{)427}$

10. $9\overline{)421}$

11. $7\overline{)686}$

12. $8\overline{)665}$

CRITICAL THINKING

Check each division problem. Are the answers correct?

1. $\dfrac{76\ \text{R}9}{64\overline{)4,873}}$

2. $\dfrac{178\ \text{R}3}{52\overline{)9,268}}$

5.6 Problem Solving: Clue Words for Division

These clue words tell you to divide.

how much did each	*how many times*
into	*how many*

READ the problem. Look for clue words. Make a PLAN. DO the plan to solve the problem.

1. A lunchroom served 960 lunches in 3 hours. The same number of lunches were served each hour. How many lunches were served each hour?

2. There are 5,040 calories in 6 cups of roasted peanuts. How many calories are there in each cup of roasted peanuts?

3. This year, the school principal ordered 2,688 books. That is 7 times the amount ordered last year. How many books were ordered last year?

4. Last week, 2,400 empty bottles were returned to the store. If a carton holds 8 bottles, how many cartons were filled?

5. There will be 1,008 people at a large banquet. Six people will sit at each table. How many tables will be filled?

6. A marching band has 120 musicians. Each row of the band has 8 musicians in it. How many rows of musicians can be made?

7. There are 288 cans of soup. These cans are to be packed into nine cases. If each case holds the same number of cans, how many cans will be in each case?

5.7 Dividing by Numbers with More Than One Digit

Divide until each digit in the dividend has been brought down.	27 R2 33)893 − 66 233 − 231 2

Divide. Some answers will have remainders.

1. 29)74

2. 28)88

3. 51)619

4. 31)99

5. 16)496

6. 45)947

7. 12)619

8. 33)699

9. 26)388

10. 15)351

11. 11)363

12. 35)696

CRITICAL THINKING

Solve the problem. Show your work.

Margot printed 378 note cards. She sold them in boxes of 12. How many boxes did she have to sell? Were any cards left over? If so, how many?

Name _____ Date _____

Sometimes, you need to place a zero in the quotient.

Divide. 5,621 ÷ 7

$$
\begin{array}{r}
803 \\
7\overline{)5621} \\
-\ 56 \\
\hline
21 \\
-\ 21 \\
\hline
0
\end{array}
$$

Divide.

1. $8\overline{)5,616}$

2. $3\overline{)3,618}$

3. $7\overline{)4,256}$

4. $6\overline{)1,842}$

5. $10\overline{)5,030}$

6. $25\overline{)7,525}$

7. $36\overline{)7,272}$

8. $15\overline{)9,045}$

9. $27\overline{)6,480}$

10. $34\overline{)8,160}$

11. $21\overline{)8,820}$

12. $18\overline{)2,880}$

CRITICAL THINKING

The answers below are incorrect. Find the error. Then show the correct division.

1. $15\overline{)6,135}$ (408 R15)

2. $12\overline{)3,672}$ (360)

5.9 Problem Solving: Choose the Operation

These clue words tell you which operation to use.			
Add	**Subtract**	**Multiply**	**Divide**
in all	*how many more*	*of*	*how many times*
total	*difference*	*at*	*into how many*
altogether	*how many fewer*	*for*	*how much did each*
both		*in each*	

READ the problem. Look for clue words. Make a PLAN. DO the plan to solve the problem.

1. A store received a shipment of car parts. One box contained 148 parts, another 132 parts, and the third 216 parts. How many car parts were received in all?

2. Together a truck and its cargo weigh 24,525 pounds. When the truck is empty, it weighs 12,750 pounds. What is the weight of the cargo?

3. There are 168 street lights along Main Street. Each light uses 225 watts of electrical power. When all the lights are on, how many watts of electrical power are being used?

4. Last year, 5,904 people attended the Hawks' home basketball games. There were 36 home games, and the same number of people attended each game. How many people attended each home game?

5. A bakery used the following amounts of milk: 9,421 kilograms, 6,125 kilograms, 8,123 kilograms, and 8,584 kilograms. What was the total amount of milk used?

6. Mount McKinley is 20,320 feet high. Mount Kennedy is 16,286 feet high. How much higher is Mount McKinley than Mount Kennedy?

▶ 5.10 Estimating and Thinking   Exercise 44

> Choose the answer that "makes sense" for the word problem.
>
> Donut Hut sold 1,764 donuts yesterday. Estimate how many dozen donuts were sold. There are 12 in a dozen.
>
> **(a)** 15   **(b)** 1,500   **(c)** 150
>
> This answer is too small.   This answer is too big.   This answer makes sense.
>
> $15 \times 12 = 180$ $1,500 \times 12 = 18,000$ $150 \times 12 = 1,800$

Choose the estimate that is close to the exact answer.

1. The New York Jets scored 666 points in one season during a total of 16 games. Estimate how many points the team scored in each game.
   (a) 10   **(b)** 100   **(c)** 40

2. Carol is sewing 41 costumes for the school play. Each costume uses the same amount of fabric. She uses 125 yards of fabric altogether. Estimate how much fabric she used for each costume.
   (a) 30 yards   **(b)** 3 yards   **(c)** 10 yards

3. Mark lifted 2 barbells with a total weight of 280 pounds. Estimate the weight of each barbell.
   (a) 14 pounds   **(b)** 1,200 pounds   **(c)** 140 pounds

4. There are 840 song titles in a jukebox. There are 120 compact discs. Estimate how many songs are on each compact disc.
   (a) 50 songs   **(b)** 900 songs   **(c)** 7 songs

5. Alice went shopping today. She spent $73.29, and she purchased 16 items of equal value. Estimate how much each item costs.
   (a) $10.00   **(b)** $2.00   **(c)** $5.00

Name _____ Date _____

 6.1 Divisibility Tests for 2, 5, and 10   **Exercise 45**

A number is **divisible by 2** if it ends in 0, 2, 4, 6, or 8.	396 ends in 6. So, 396 is divisible by 2.

Tell if each number is divisible by 2. Write *Yes* or *No*.

1. 0 _____   **2.** 1 _____   **3.** 100 _____   **4.** 2,916 _____

5. 49 _____   **6.** 358 _____   **7.** 3,792 _____   **8.** 1,003 _____

A number is **divisible by 5** if it ends in 0 or 5.	225 ends in 5. So, 225 is divisible by 5.
A number is **divisible by 10** if it ends in 0.	520 ends in 0. So, 520 is divisible by 10.

Tell if each number is divisible by 5, 10, or both 5 and 10.

9. 10 _____   **10.** 3,005 _____   **11.** 5,550 _____   **12.** 23,095 _____

Tell if each number is divisible by 2, 5, 10, or all of the numbers.

13. 165 _____   **14.** 5,554 _____   **15.** 6,000 _____   **16.** 426,805 _____

CRITICAL THINKING

Find a number that is divisible by:

1. 2 and not 5   **2.** 5 and not 10   **3.** 2 and 5

6.2 Divisibility Tests for 3, 6, and 9 **Exercise 46**

A number is **divisible by 3** if the **sum of its digits** is divisible by 3.	$456 \rightarrow 4 + 5 + 6 = 15$ 15 is divisible by 3. So, 456 is divisible by 3.

A number is **divisible by 6** if it is divisible by **both 2 and 3.**

Tell if each number is divisible by 6. Write *Yes* or *No*.

1. 60 _____   **2.** 75 _____   **3.** 642 _____   **4.** 662 _____

5. 4,323 _____   6. 486 _____   **7.** 3,000 _____   **8.** 6,666 _____

A number is **divisible by 9** if the **sum of its digits** is divisible by 9.	$864 \rightarrow 8 + 6 + 4 = 18$ 18 is divisible by 9. So, 486 is divisible by 9.

Tell if each number is divisible by 3, 9, or both 3 and 9.

9. 30 _____   **10.** 90 _____   **11.** 993 _____   **12.** 768 _____

13. 102 _____   **14.** 9,009 _____   **15.** 38,109 _____   **16.** 57,249 _____

CRITICAL THINKING

Find a number that is divisible by:

1. 3 and not 2   **2.** 9 and not 6

3. Can you find a number that is divisible by 9 and not 3? Why or why not?

▶ 6.3 Divisibility Test for 4   Exercise 47

> A number is **divisible by 4** if the number formed by the
> **last two digits** is divisible by 4.
>
> 680   3,900
> 80 is divisible by 4.   00 is divisible by 4.
> So, 680 is divisible by 4.   So, 3,900 is divisible by 4.

Tell if each number is divisible by 4. Write *Yes* or *No*.

1. 396 _____   **2.** 386 _____   **3.** 70 _____   **4.** 60 _____

5. 100 _____   **6.** 912 _____   **7.** 704 _____   **8.** 694 _____

9. 4,862 _____   **10.** 2,550 _____   **11.** 964 _____   **12.** 124,446 _____

13. 7,008 _____   **14.** 16,748 _____   **15.** 345,032 _____   **16.** 728,139 _____

CRITICAL THINKING

In a 200-mile bike race, there are medical stations every
4 miles. Of the following mile markers, circle the ones that
will have medical stations.

16   29   50   74   100   144   186   196

6.4 Factors and Greatest Common Factor   Exercise 48

For a number to be a factor, the division must have a remainder of 0.

Divide to find the factors of 24.

$$\frac{24}{1)24} \qquad \frac{12}{2)24} \qquad \frac{8}{3)24} \qquad \frac{6}{4)24} \qquad \frac{4 \ R4}{5)24} \qquad \frac{4}{6)24} \ \text{Stop}$$

The factors of 24 are 1, 2, 3, 4, 6, 8, 12, and 24.

Find the factors of each number.

1. 30 _____   **2.** 16 _____   **3.** 18 _____

4. 26 _____   **5.** 45 _____   **6.** 22 _____

The **greatest common factor** is the largest common factor.

Factors of 12 = {1, 2, 3, 4, 6, 12}
Factors of 18 = {1, 2 ,3, 6, 9, 18}

The greatest common factor of 12 and 18 is 6.

Find the greatest common factor of each pair of numbers.

7. 6   10   **8.** 12   20   **9.** 24   25   **10.** 20   16

11. 18   30   **12.** 40   50   **13.** 45   90   **14.** 99   11

CRITICAL THINKING

What is the greatest common factor of 18, 36, and 48?

6.5 Multiples and Least Common Multiple   Exercise 49

Multiply to find the **least common multiple** of 8 and 12.

Multiples of 8 = {8, 16, **24**, 32, 40...}
Multiples of 12 = {12, **24**, 36...}

The least common multiple of 8 and 12 is **24**.

Write the first five multiples of each number. List them from least to greatest.

1. 6 _____

2. 12 _____

3. 20 _____

4. 16 _____

5. 25 _____

6. 9 _____

Find the least common multiple for each pair of numbers.

7. 4   5

8. 6   9

9. 2   9

10. 12   48

11. 12   16

12. 25   10

13. 15   12

14. 20   50

CRITICAL THINKING

A lighthouse flashes a red light every 6 minutes and a green light every 9 minutes. At 7:00 P.M., the lighthouse flashes the red and green lights at the same time. Name the next three times that the lighthouse will flash the red and green lights at the same time.

▶ 6.6 Prime Numbers   Exercise 50

A **composite number** has more than two factors.
A **prime number** has only two factors: itself and 1.

The **prime factorization** of a number uses only factors that
are prime numbers. You can use a factor tree to find the prime
factorization of 20.

$$20$$
$$2 \times 10$$
$$2 \times 5$$

The prime factorization of 20 is $2 \times 2 \times 5$.

Tell if each number is *prime* or *composite*.

1. 9 _____   **2.** 23 _____   **3.** 21 _____   **4.** 17 _____

Write the prime factorization of each number. Use a factor tree.

5. 10   **6.** 21   **7.** 28

8. 36   **9.** 48   **10.** 90

CRITICAL THINKING

Find the prime for factorization of the number 24 in
three different ways. Show that the prime factorization
is always the same.

◢ 6.7 Exponents   Exercise 51

An exponent tells you how many times the number is used as a factor.

Find the value of 5^3. $5^3 = 5 \times 5 \times 5 = 125$

Any number with a zero exponent equals 1.

Find the value of 5^0. $5^0 = 1$

Find the value of each expression.

1. $3^2 =$ _____   2. $11^1 =$ _____   3. $2^4 =$ _____   4. $4^2 =$ _____

5. $3^4 =$ _____   6. $4^3 =$ _____   7. $46^0 =$ _____   8. $25^2 =$ _____

9. $8^3 -$ _____   10. $11^2 =$ _____   11. $21^1 =$ _____   12. $30^3 =$ _____

13. $8^4 =$ _____   14. $40^2 =$ _____   15. $6^4 =$ _____   16. $2^3 =$ _____

CRITICAL THINKING

Decide what the missing number should be to make each statement true.
Then rewrite the statement with the exponent.

1. $25 = 5^{\blacksquare}$ 2. $81 = 3^{\blacksquare}$

3. $32 = 2^{\blacksquare}$ 4. $1 = 400^{\blacksquare}$

5. $10,000 = 10^{\blacksquare}$ 6. $900 = 30^{\blacksquare}$

Name _____ Date _____

6.8 Squares and Square Roots

Find the square of 8.	$8^2 = 8 \times 8 = 64$
Find the square root of 900.	$10 \times 10 = 100$ too small
	$20 \times 20 = 400$ too small
	$30 \times 30 = 900$
	$\sqrt{900} = 30$ ✓

Find the square of each number.

1. $1^2 =$ _____   **2.** $10^2 =$ _____   **3.** $5^2 =$ _____   **4.** $6^2 =$ _____   **5.** $11^2 =$ _____

6. $12^2 =$ _____   **7.** $9^2 =$ _____   **8.** $15^2 =$ _____   **9.** $7^2 =$ _____   **10.** $40^2 =$ _____

Find the square root of each number.

11. $\sqrt{9} =$ _____   **12.** $\sqrt{81} =$ _____   **13.** $\sqrt{169} =$ _____   **14.** $\sqrt{225} =$ _____   **15.** $\sqrt{49} =$ _____

16. $\sqrt{100} =$ _____   **17.** $\sqrt{400} =$ _____   **18.** $\sqrt{64} =$ _____   **19.** $\sqrt{144} =$ _____   **20.** $\sqrt{196} =$ _____

CRITICAL THINKING

Use the picture to answer the questions.

1. How many squares are on the side of the figure?

2. How many squares are on the bottom of the figure?

3. How many squares are there in all?

4. $3^2 =$

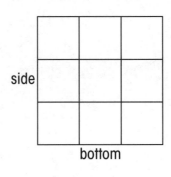

side

bottom

▶ 6.9 Problem Solving: Extra Information   **Exercise 53**

> Remember to use only the information you need.
>
> Ms. Aird supervises 50 employees and their accounts. Each employee works 40 hours a week and is responsible for three accounts. How many accounts does Ms. Aird supervise altogether?
>
> **PLAN**   What information do you need?
> number of employees   50
> number of accounts   3
> Multiply to find the number of accounts altogether.
>
> **DO**   Multiply. $50 \times 3 = 150$
>
> Ms. Aird supervises 150 accounts.

READ the problem. Make a PLAN. DO the plan to solve the problem.

1. There were 2,500 people at the Thanksgiving Day football game. The sophomore class sold 450 programs for $2 each. How much money did the class make selling programs?

2. It snowed on 12 days out of 30. Each time it snowed, about 2 inches fell. How many inches of snow fell over the 30 days?

3. Ray hiked for 5 hours and covered 12 miles. Along the way, he passed 60 trail markers. About how many trail markers did he pass in each mile that he hiked?

4. Kelly drove 1,200 miles over 3 days. She used 40 gallons of gas for the trip. How many miles did she drive on each gallon?

5. To paint his apartment, Evan bought 6 cans of white paint and 2 cans of green paint. The green paint was on sale. He can paint one room with two cans of paint. How many rooms can he paint altogether?

▶ 7.1 What Is a Fraction?   **Exercise 54**

Write a fraction to tell what part of the figure is shaded.

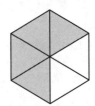

$\dfrac{4}{6}$ Shaded parts
     Total parts

Four-sixths of the figure is shaded.

Write a fraction to tell what part of each figure is shaded.

1.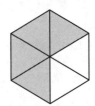

2.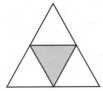

3.

4.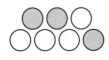

5.

6.

CRITICAL THINKING

Does the shaded part of the square show $\dfrac{1}{4}$? Explain your answer.

Name _____ Date _____

▶ 7.2 Recognizing Equivalent Fractions   Exercise 55

Three equivalent fractions
are pictured below.

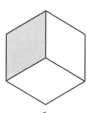 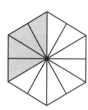

$$\frac{1}{3} \ = \ \frac{2}{6} \ = \ \frac{4}{12}$$

Tell if each pair of fractions is equivalent. Write *Equivalent* or *Not equivalent*.

1.

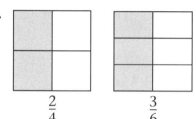

$\frac{2}{4}$ $\frac{3}{6}$

2.

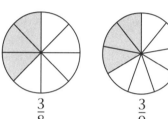

$\frac{3}{8}$ $\frac{3}{9}$

3.

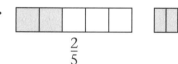

$\frac{2}{5}$ $\frac{4}{10}$

4.

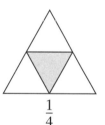

$\frac{1}{4}$ $\frac{2}{8}$

5.

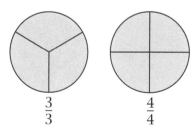

$\frac{3}{3}$ $\frac{4}{4}$

6.

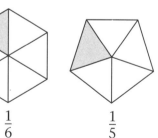

$\frac{1}{6}$ $\frac{1}{5}$

CRITICAL THINKING

Draw a picture to help you answer the question.

Anna cut her apple pie into four slices and ate one slice.
Lisa cut her apple pie into eight slices and ate two slices.
Draw each apple pie. Shade each piece that was eaten.
Did Anna and Lisa eat the same amount of pie?

▶ 7.3 Reducing Fractions to Lowest Terms   Exercise 56

To reduce a fraction to lowest terms, divide the numerator and denominator by the greatest common factor.

Reduce $\frac{12}{20}$ to lowest terms.

Factors of 12 = {1, 2, 3, **4**, 6, 12}

Factors of 20 = {1, 2, **4**, 5, 10, 20}

Greatest Common Factor = 4

$\frac{12 \div 4}{20 \div 4} = \frac{3}{5}$

Decide if each fraction is reduced to lowest terms. Write *Yes* or *No*.

1. $\frac{2}{5}$ _____   **2.** $\frac{4}{6}$ _____   **3.** $\frac{7}{12}$ _____   **4.** $\frac{4}{15}$ _____

Reduce each fraction to lowest terms.

5. $\frac{8}{12} =$ **6.** $\frac{8}{8} =$ **7.** $\frac{6}{8} =$ **8.** $\frac{10}{15} =$

9. $\frac{12}{15} =$ **10.** $\frac{9}{15} =$ **11.** $\frac{2}{6} =$ **12.** $\frac{9}{12} =$

13. $\frac{8}{10} =$ **14.** $\frac{8}{20} =$ **15.** $\frac{12}{18} =$ **16.** $\frac{20}{50} =$

17. $\frac{6}{18} =$ **18.** $\frac{18}{24} =$ **19.** $\frac{16}{48} =$ **20.** $\frac{10}{24} =$

CRITICAL THINKING

Solve the problem. Show your work.

There are 100 cents in a dollar. What fraction of a dollar is 25 cents? Write the fraction in lowest terms.

Name _____   Date _____

▶ 7.4 Changing Fractions to Higher Terms   Exercise 57

To write a fraction in higher terms, multiply the numerator and denominator by the same number.

$$\frac{5}{6} = \frac{?}{18}$$

$$18 \div 6 = 3$$

$$\frac{5 \times 3}{6 \times 3} = \frac{15}{18}$$

$$\frac{5}{6} = \frac{15}{18}$$

Change each fraction to higher terms. Use the higher denominator shown.

1. $\frac{1}{2} = \frac{?}{12}$ 2. $\frac{2}{3} = \frac{?}{15}$ 3. $\frac{4}{5} = \frac{?}{20}$ 4. $\frac{3}{4} = \frac{?}{8}$

5. $\frac{1}{7} = \frac{?}{21}$ 6. $\frac{3}{10} = \frac{?}{40}$ 7. $\frac{5}{8} = \frac{?}{24}$ 8. $\frac{2}{9} = \frac{?}{18}$

9. $\frac{5}{16} = \frac{?}{48}$ 10. $\frac{7}{8} = \frac{?}{32}$ 11. $\frac{1}{4} = \frac{?}{16}$ 12. $\frac{5}{9} = \frac{?}{36}$

13. $\frac{3}{4} = \frac{?}{20}$ 14. $\frac{3}{5} = \frac{?}{25}$ 15. $\frac{9}{10} = \frac{?}{30}$ 16. $\frac{2}{3} = \frac{?}{18}$

17. $\frac{1}{5} = \frac{?}{100}$ 18. $\frac{1}{4} = \frac{?}{100}$ 19. $\frac{2}{3} = \frac{?}{75}$ 20. $\frac{1}{6} = \frac{?}{36}$

CRITICAL THINKING

Find the missing numerator or denominator that makes each pair of fractions equivalent.

1. $\frac{3}{?} = \frac{9}{15}$ 2. $\frac{4}{5} = \frac{20}{?}$ 3. $\frac{?}{18} = \frac{5}{6}$

▶ 7.5 Finding Common Denominators   Exercise 58

To change unlike fractions to like fractions, remember to first find a common denominator.

Change $\frac{5}{6}$ and $\frac{4}{9}$ to like fractions.

Multiples of 6 : {6, 12, **18**, . . .}
Multiples of 9 : {9, **18**, . . .}
Least common multiple = 18

$$\frac{5 \times 3}{6 \times 3} = \frac{15}{18} \qquad \frac{4 \times 2}{9 \times 2} = \frac{8}{18}$$

The fractions $\frac{15}{18}$ and $\frac{8}{18}$ are like fractions.

Change each pair of fractions to like fractions.

1. $\frac{1}{5}$ $\frac{2}{3}$

2. $\frac{3}{4}$ $\frac{3}{10}$

3. $\frac{4}{9}$ $\frac{5}{12}$

4. $\frac{3}{8}$ $\frac{1}{12}$

5. $\frac{1}{6}$ $\frac{3}{10}$

6. $\frac{1}{3}$ $\frac{3}{4}$

7. $\frac{2}{3}$ $\frac{1}{9}$

8. $\frac{5}{8}$ $\frac{5}{6}$

9. $\frac{1}{6}$ $\frac{4}{9}$

10. $\frac{7}{10}$ $\frac{4}{15}$

CRITICAL THINKING

A quarter is $\frac{1}{4}$ of a dollar. A nickel is $\frac{1}{20}$ of a dollar. A dime is $\frac{1}{10}$ of a dollar. Write these fractions as like fractions with a denominator of 100.

▶ 7.6 Comparing Fractions   Exercise 59

To compare fractions, change all fractions to like fractions. Then, compare the numerators.

Compare $\frac{3}{8}$ and $\frac{5}{12}$.

$$\frac{3 \times 3}{8 \times 3} = \frac{9}{24} \qquad \frac{5 \times 2}{12 \times 2} = \frac{10}{24}$$

$$\frac{9}{24} < \frac{10}{24}$$

$$\frac{3}{8} \ < \ \frac{5}{12}$$

Compare each pair of fractions. Use >, <, or =.

1. $\frac{2}{5}$ $\frac{3}{5}$ 2. $\frac{3}{4}$ $\frac{2}{4}$ 3. $\frac{4}{10}$ $\frac{3}{10}$

4. $\frac{2}{5}$ $\frac{2}{4}$ 5. $\frac{1}{6}$ $\frac{2}{9}$ 6. $\frac{5}{8}$ $\frac{3}{7}$

7. $\frac{2}{3}$ $\frac{6}{9}$ 8. $\frac{4}{20}$ $\frac{4}{25}$ 9. $\frac{5}{12}$ $\frac{1}{3}$

10. $\frac{4}{5}$ $\frac{3}{15}$ 11. $\frac{7}{10}$ $\frac{3}{4}$ 12. $\frac{2}{3}$ $\frac{6}{10}$

13. $\frac{1}{5}$ $\frac{3}{20}$ 14. $\frac{7}{18}$ $\frac{3}{9}$ 15. $\frac{3}{15}$ $\frac{5}{20}$

CRITICAL THINKING

Find the missing numerator to make each comparison true.

1. $\frac{4}{5} > \frac{?}{5}$ 2. $\frac{2}{3} < \frac{?}{9}$ 3. $\frac{?}{4} < \frac{2}{3}$

7.7 Ordering Fractions

To order fractions, you must use like fractions.

Write these fractions in order from least to greatest: $\frac{1}{4}$ $\frac{1}{5}$ $\frac{3}{10}$

A common multiple of 4, 5, and 10 is 20. Use 20 as the common denominator.

$\frac{1 \times 5}{4 \times 5} = \frac{5}{20}$ $\qquad$ $\frac{1 \times 4}{5 \times 4} = \frac{4}{20}$ $\qquad$ $\frac{3 \times 2}{10 \times 2} = \frac{6}{20}$

The fractions in order are $\frac{1}{5}$ $\frac{1}{4}$ $\frac{3}{10}$.

Write the fractions in order from least to greatest.

1. $\frac{2}{3}$ $\frac{3}{8}$ $\frac{1}{4}$ $\qquad$ 2. $\frac{3}{4}$ $\frac{4}{5}$ $\frac{7}{10}$ $\qquad$ 3. $\frac{5}{8}$ $\frac{5}{6}$ $\frac{9}{12}$

4. $\frac{5}{9}$ $\frac{1}{4}$ $\frac{7}{12}$ $\qquad$ 5. $\frac{1}{3}$ $\frac{5}{24}$ $\frac{4}{6}$ $\qquad$ 6. $\frac{4}{5}$ $\frac{3}{12}$ $\frac{5}{6}$

7. $\frac{9}{16}$ $\frac{1}{3}$ $\frac{7}{24}$ $\qquad$ 8. $\frac{1}{2}$ $\frac{3}{5}$ $\frac{4}{7}$ $\qquad$ 9. $\frac{5}{6}$ $\frac{5}{8}$ $\frac{5}{9}$

10. $\frac{4}{15}$ $\frac{1}{3}$ $\frac{3}{10}$ $\qquad$ 11. $\frac{6}{25}$ $\frac{4}{10}$ $\frac{7}{20}$ $\qquad$ 12. $\frac{4}{12}$ $\frac{3}{15}$ $\frac{7}{30}$

CRITICAL THINKING

Mrs. Delgado bought $\frac{1}{5}$ pound turkey, $\frac{3}{4}$ pound of cheese, and $\frac{1}{2}$ pound of bologna. Write the amount of each food in order from the greatest amount to the least amount.

▶ 7.8 Changing Fractions to Mixed Numbers

Exercise 61

Divide to change improper fractions to mixed numbers.

Change $\frac{18}{4}$ to a mixed number.

$$4\frac{2}{4} = 4\frac{1}{2}$$
$$4\overline{)18}$$
$$\underline{-16}$$
$$2$$

Change each fraction to a mixed number or a whole number.

1. $\frac{8}{2} =$ **2.** $\frac{12}{5} =$ **3.** $\frac{15}{7} =$ **4.** $\frac{22}{5} =$

5. $\frac{33}{4} =$ **6.** $\frac{17}{3} =$ **7.** $\frac{25}{5} =$ **8.** $\frac{19}{4} =$

9. $\frac{24}{10} =$ **10.** $\frac{38}{6} =$ **11.** $\frac{60}{12} =$ **12.** $\frac{45}{10} =$

13. $\frac{39}{8} =$ **14.** $\frac{44}{11} =$ **15.** $\frac{48}{9} =$ **16.** $\frac{20}{3} =$

17. $\frac{42}{4} =$ **18.** $\frac{72}{9} =$ **19.** $\frac{56}{13} =$ **20.** $\frac{48}{12} =$

CRITICAL THINKING

Lui has 7 sticks of butter. Each stick is $\frac{1}{4}$ pound.
How many whole pounds of butter does he have?

7.9 Changing Mixed Numbers to Fractions

Exercise 62

> To change mixed numbers to improper fractions, multiply the denominator of the fraction by the whole number. Then, add the numerator of the fraction to the product. Keep the denominator the same.
>
> Change $2\frac{1}{3}$ to an improper fraction.
> $2 \times 3 = 6$
> $6 + 1 = 7$
> $2\frac{1}{3} = \frac{7}{3}$

Change each mixed number or whole number to an improper fraction.

1. $5\frac{1}{3} =$ **2.** $6\frac{2}{5} =$ **3.** $1\frac{1}{4} =$

4. $3 =$ **5.** $4\frac{3}{8} =$ **6.** $4\frac{1}{2} =$

7. $8\frac{1}{5} =$ **8.** $9\frac{2}{3} =$ **9.** $10 =$

10. $7\frac{3}{10} =$ **11.** $6\frac{5}{9} =$ **12.** $4\frac{1}{5} =$

13. $2\frac{3}{11} =$ **14.** $12\frac{4}{5} =$ **15.** $8\frac{1}{8} =$

16. $10\frac{1}{2} =$ **17.** $4\frac{3}{15} =$ **18.** $7\frac{3}{7} =$

CRITICAL THINKING

Joey saved $5\frac{3}{4}$ dollars in quarters. Write $5\frac{3}{4}$ as an improper fraction. How many quarters did Joey save?

▶ 7.10 Ordering Numbers You Know   Exercise 63

> To put numbers in order, change improper fractions to mixed numbers. Find like fractions if necessary.
>
> Write the numbers in order from least to greatest: $\frac{7}{3}$ $\frac{5}{2}$ 2
>
>   Change to mixed like numbers
>
> $\frac{7}{3} = 2\frac{1}{3} = 2\frac{2}{6}$
>
> $\frac{5}{2} = 2\frac{1}{2} = 2\frac{3}{6}$ ← greatest
>
> $2 = 2 = 2$ ← least
>
> The numbers in order from least to greatest are: 2, $\frac{7}{3}$, $\frac{5}{2}$.

Write each group of numbers in order from least to greatest.

1. 5 $\frac{5}{7}$ $\frac{7}{5}$

2. 4 $\frac{16}{4}$ $\frac{8}{2}$

3. 3 $2\frac{1}{3}$ $\frac{5}{2}$

4. $\frac{4}{5}$ $\frac{5}{4}$ $\frac{2}{5}$

5. 5 $\frac{9}{5}$ $1\frac{3}{5}$

6. $\frac{11}{8}$ $\frac{5}{4}$ 2

7. $\frac{15}{4}$ 3 $\frac{7}{2}$

8. $2\frac{5}{6}$ $3\frac{1}{3}$ $\frac{13}{6}$

9. $\frac{8}{3}$ $\frac{6}{3}$ $\frac{3}{2}$

10. $\frac{10}{4}$ $\frac{7}{4}$ 4

CRITICAL THINKING

1. Make a fraction that is between 1 and 2.

2. Make a fraction that is between $\frac{3}{5}$ and 1.

3. Make a fraction that has a denominator of 3 and is greater than 1.

Name _____ Date _____

7.11 Problem Solving: Patterns   Exercise 64

To complete this sequence, use a commom denominator.

$$\frac{1}{12}, \frac{1}{6}, \underline{\quad}, \frac{1}{3}, \frac{5}{12}, \underline{\quad}, \underline{\quad}$$

Use 12 as a common denominator. $\frac{1}{12}, \frac{2}{12}, \underline{\quad}, \frac{4}{12}, \frac{5}{12}, \underline{\quad}, \underline{\quad}$

Look for a pattern and complete it. $\frac{1}{12}, \frac{2}{12}, \frac{3}{12}, \frac{4}{12}, \frac{5}{12}, \frac{6}{12}, \frac{7}{12}$

Reduce to lowest terms, where needed.

The complete sequence is: $\frac{1}{12}, \frac{1}{6}, \frac{1}{4}, \frac{1}{3}, \frac{5}{12}, \frac{1}{2}, \frac{7}{12}, \frac{3}{4}$

Complete each sequence. Write each fraction in lowest terms.

1. $\frac{1}{2}, 1, \frac{3}{2}, 2, \underline{\quad}, \underline{\quad}, 3\frac{1}{2}, \underline{\quad}$

2. $\frac{1}{4}, \frac{5}{12}, \frac{7}{12}, \underline{\quad}, \underline{\quad}, \underline{\quad}, 1\frac{1}{4}$

3. $\frac{3}{4}, 1\frac{1}{2}, 2\frac{1}{4}, 3, \underline{\quad}, 4\frac{1}{2}, \underline{\quad}, \underline{\quad}$

4. $2, 1\frac{3}{4}, 1\frac{1}{2}, 1\frac{1}{4}, \underline{\quad}, \underline{\quad}, \underline{\quad}$

5. $1\frac{1}{2}, 3, 4\frac{1}{2}, \underline{\quad}, 7\frac{1}{2}, \underline{\quad}, 10\frac{1}{2}, \underline{\quad}$

6. $\frac{1}{20}, \frac{1}{10}, \frac{3}{20}, \frac{1}{5}, \underline{\quad}, \underline{\quad}, \underline{\quad}$

CRITICAL THINKING

Explain the pattern in each of the sequences.

1. $0, \frac{1}{2}, \frac{1}{2}, 1, 1\frac{1}{2}, 2\frac{1}{2}, 4$

2. $\frac{1}{2}, \frac{1}{4}, \frac{1}{16}, \frac{1}{256}$

64 Chapter 7 • Understanding Fractions and Mixed Numbers

Copyright © by Globe Fearon, Inc. All rights reserved.

▶ 8.1 Multiplying Fractions   Exercise 65

To multiply fractions, multiply the numerators. Then, multiply the denominators. Reduce the answer to lowest terms, if possible.

Multiply. $\frac{1}{6} \times \frac{2}{3}$ $\frac{1}{6} \times \frac{2}{3} = \frac{2}{18}$

$\frac{2 \div 2}{18 \div 2} = \frac{1}{9}$ ← lowest terms

Multiply. Write each product in lowest terms.

1. $\frac{1}{2} \times \frac{3}{5} =$ **2.** $\frac{3}{4} \times \frac{1}{4} =$ **3.** $\frac{4}{5} \times \frac{3}{7} =$ **4.** $\frac{3}{10} \times \frac{2}{5} =$

5. $\frac{3}{4} \times \frac{1}{2} =$ **6.** $\frac{7}{8} \times \frac{2}{3} =$ **7.** $\frac{2}{9} \times \frac{3}{4} =$ **8.** $\frac{3}{7} \times \frac{5}{6} =$

9. $\frac{1}{8} \times \frac{8}{9} =$ **10.** $\frac{1}{3} \times \frac{3}{5} =$ **11.** $\frac{3}{8} \times \frac{3}{8} =$ **12.** $\frac{4}{9} \times \frac{1}{4} =$

13. $\frac{4}{9} \times \frac{1}{2} =$ **14.** $\frac{3}{5} \times \frac{3}{10} =$ **15.** $\frac{2}{3} \times \frac{3}{4} =$ **16.** $\frac{5}{8} \times \frac{2}{3} =$

CRITICAL THINKING

1. What is $\frac{1}{2} \times \frac{3}{4}$? Look at the grid on the right to find the product.

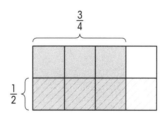

2. What is $\frac{2}{3} \times \frac{1}{4}$? Shade the grid on the right to show the product.

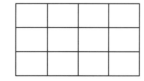

8.2 Canceling

Remember to cancel fractions whenever you can before multiplying.

Multiply. $\dfrac{4}{9} \times \dfrac{6}{7}$

Divide both the numerator 6 and the denominator 9 by 3.

$$\dfrac{4}{\overset{}{\underset{3}{\cancel{9}}}} \times \dfrac{\overset{2}{\cancel{6}}}{7} = \dfrac{8}{21}$$

Multiply. Remember to cancel before you multiply.

1. $\dfrac{2}{5} \times \dfrac{5}{12} =$ **2.** $\dfrac{4}{9} \times \dfrac{3}{8} =$ **3.** $\dfrac{2}{3} \times \dfrac{3}{4} =$ **4.** $\dfrac{4}{15} \times \dfrac{5}{12} =$

5. $\dfrac{1}{2} \times \dfrac{4}{9} =$ **6.** $\dfrac{6}{7} \times \dfrac{2}{3} =$ **7.** $\dfrac{4}{12} \times \dfrac{9}{16} =$ **8.** $\dfrac{1}{4} \times \dfrac{4}{11} =$

9. $\dfrac{3}{4} \times \dfrac{2}{15} =$ **10.** $\dfrac{5}{18} \times \dfrac{9}{10} =$ **11.** $\dfrac{5}{9} \times \dfrac{1}{5} =$ **12.** $\dfrac{8}{15} \times \dfrac{5}{8} =$

13. $\dfrac{3}{5} \times \dfrac{10}{21} =$ **14.** $\dfrac{3}{16} \times \dfrac{4}{15} =$ **15.** $\dfrac{5}{6} \times \dfrac{3}{10} =$ **16.** $\dfrac{7}{15} \times \dfrac{10}{21} =$

CRITICAL THINKING

Find the missing number in each multiplication problem.

1. $\dfrac{4}{\underset{3}{\blacksquare}} \times \dfrac{\overset{1}{\cancel{3}}}{5} = \dfrac{4}{15}$

2. $\dfrac{\overset{1}{\blacksquare}}{\underset{3}{\blacksquare}} \times \dfrac{\overset{2}{\cancel{4}}}{\underset{1}{\cancel{3}}} = \dfrac{2}{3}$

Name _____ Date _____

8.3 Multiplying Fractions and Whole Numbers

Exercise 67

To multiply fractions and whole numbers, first change the whole number to a fraction. Place the whole number over 1.

Multiply. $30 \times \frac{5}{12}$

$$\frac{\overset{5}{\cancel{30}}}{1} \times \frac{5}{\underset{2}{\cancel{12}}} = \frac{25}{2} = 12\frac{1}{2}$$

Multiply. Cancel, if possible.

1. $\frac{3}{8} \times 16 =$ **2.** $14 \times \frac{3}{4} =$ **3.** $\frac{1}{5} \times 22 =$ **4.** $\frac{1}{8} \times 8 =$

5. $\frac{1}{2} \times 10 =$ **6.** $\frac{2}{3} \times 9 =$ **7.** $15 \times \frac{3}{10} =$ **8.** $7 \times \frac{2}{7} =$

9. $\frac{5}{12} \times 48 =$ **10.** $20 \times \frac{3}{8} =$ **11.** $\frac{3}{4} \times 16 =$ **12.** $\frac{1}{8} \times 12 =$

13. $30 \times \frac{5}{8} =$ **14.** $10 \times \frac{3}{4} =$ **15.** $\frac{1}{9} \times 45 =$ **16.** $\frac{7}{8} \times 24 =$

CRITICAL THINKING

Solve each problem. Show your work.

1. A survey asked 50 dentists to tell what brand of toothpaste they like to use. Of the dentists surveyed, $\frac{4}{5}$ said they liked Socleen. How many dentists said they liked Socleen?

2. In a class of 18 students, $\frac{2}{3}$ of them speak two languages. How many students speak two languages?

8.4 Multiplying Mixed Numbers   Exercise 68

Before multiplying mixed numbers and whole numbers, first change the mixed numbers to improper fractions.

Multiply. $3\frac{2}{5} \times 1\frac{2}{3}$ $\frac{17}{\cancel{5}_{1}} \times \frac{\cancel{5}^{1}}{3} = \frac{17}{3} = 5\frac{2}{3}$

Multiply. Cancel, if possible.

1. $3\frac{1}{2} \times 8 =$ **2.** $1\frac{1}{3} \times 1\frac{1}{5} =$ **3.** $4\frac{1}{2} \times 3\frac{1}{6} =$ **4.** $\frac{3}{5} \times 1\frac{3}{4} =$

5. $2\frac{3}{4} \times \frac{4}{11} =$ **6.** $20 \times 4\frac{2}{5} =$ **7.** $5\frac{1}{3} \times 3\frac{3}{8} =$ **8.** $6 \times 5\frac{1}{3} =$

9. $3\frac{1}{2} \times \frac{2}{7} =$ **10.** $1\frac{1}{2} \times 15 =$ **11.** $1\frac{4}{9} \times \frac{1}{3} =$ **12.** $25 \times 2\frac{1}{5} =$

13. $5\frac{1}{2} \times 2 =$ **14.** $4\frac{5}{9} \times 1\frac{1}{2} =$ **15.** $2\frac{3}{7} \times 28 =$ **16.** $2\frac{2}{3} \times 1\frac{1}{8} =$

CRITICAL THINKING

Solve each problem. Show your work.

1. On Friday, the stock price of Earth Slick was $6. On Monday, the price was $2\frac{1}{2}$ times Friday's price. What was Monday's price?

2. The park covers $7\frac{1}{4}$ acres. $\frac{1}{3}$ of the park is water. How many acres of the park are water?

Date _____

▶ 8.5 Dividing by Fractions   **Exercise 69**

> To divide by a fraction, invert the second number. Then, multiply.
>
> Divide. $\dfrac{2}{3} \div \dfrac{3}{4}$ $\dfrac{2}{3} \div \dfrac{3}{4}$
>
> $\dfrac{2}{3} \times \dfrac{4}{3} = \dfrac{8}{9}$

Divide. Write each answer in lowest terms.

1. $5 \div \dfrac{1}{6} =$ **2.** $12 \div \dfrac{1}{2} =$ **3.** $10 \div \dfrac{2}{5} =$ **4.** $\dfrac{1}{3} \div \dfrac{1}{4} =$

5. $\dfrac{3}{4} \div \dfrac{3}{4} =$ **6.** $\dfrac{1}{4} \div \dfrac{1}{2} =$ **7.** $\dfrac{3}{5} \div \dfrac{1}{5} =$ **8.** $\dfrac{4}{7} \div \dfrac{4}{5} =$

9. $\dfrac{4}{5} \div \dfrac{2}{3} =$ **10.** $\dfrac{7}{9} \div \dfrac{2}{3} -$ **11.** $\dfrac{2}{13} \div \dfrac{1}{26} =$ **12.** $1 \div \dfrac{2}{3} =$

13. $\dfrac{3}{8} \div \dfrac{3}{10} =$ **14.** $\dfrac{3}{10} \div \dfrac{3}{8} =$ **15.** $\dfrac{5}{6} \div \dfrac{1}{6} =$ **16.** $\dfrac{2}{3} \div \dfrac{8}{9} =$

CRITICAL THINKING

1. How many $\dfrac{1}{4}$ pounds are there in 2 pounds?

2. How many $\dfrac{1}{4}$ inches are there in $\dfrac{3}{4}$ inch?

3. How many $\dfrac{1}{4}$ hours are there in $\dfrac{1}{2}$ hour?

4. How many $\dfrac{1}{2}$ gallons are there in $1\dfrac{1}{2}$ gallons?

8.6 Dividing Fraction by Whole Numbers   Exercise 70

When dividing by a whole number, change the whole number to an improper fraction.

Divide. $\frac{4}{5} \div 8$

$$\frac{4}{5} \div \frac{8}{1}$$

$$\frac{\overset{1}{\cancel{4}}}{5} \times \frac{1}{\cancel{8}_2} = \frac{1}{10}$$

Divide. Remember to invert the second number and multiply.

1. $\frac{4}{5} \div 4 =$ 2. $\frac{6}{7} \div 3 =$ 3. $\frac{2}{5} \div 10 =$ 4. $5 \div \frac{2}{5} =$

5. $\frac{7}{9} \div 1 =$ 6. $\frac{5}{12} \div 10 =$ 7. $\frac{1}{2} \div 5 =$ 8. $5 \div \frac{1}{2} =$

9. $\frac{7}{8} \div 7 =$ 10. $\frac{3}{8} \div 12 =$ 11. $\frac{2}{3} \div 6 =$ 12. $\frac{4}{9} \div 8 =$

13. $\frac{7}{12} \div 14 =$ 14. $\frac{1}{8} \div 10 =$ 15. $10 \div \frac{1}{8} =$ 16. $\frac{3}{4} \div 12 =$

CRITICAL THINKING

Write the original division problem for each answer.

1. $\blacksquare \div \blacksquare = \frac{1}{3} \times \frac{3}{2} = \frac{1}{2}$

2. $\blacksquare \div \blacksquare = \frac{5}{6} \times 6 = 5$

3. $\blacksquare \div \blacksquare = \frac{3}{10} \times \frac{5}{2} = \frac{3}{4}$

▶ 8.7 Problem Solving: Exercise 71
Solve a Simpler Problem

Use whole numbers to help you decide which operation to use.

Craig has 6 yards of fabric. He needs $\frac{3}{4}$ yard to make a shirt. How many shirts can he make?

PLAN Pretend that he needs 2 yards to make a shirt. How many shirts can he make? What would you do to find out? Divide.   6 yards ÷ 2 yards = ?

DO Replace 2 yards with $\frac{3}{4}$ yard. Then divide. 6 yards ÷ $\frac{3}{4}$ yards = 8 shirts

Craig can make 8 shirts.

READ the problem. Replace the fraction with a whole number. Make a PLAN. Use the original numbers to DO the plan.

1. Indirah spends 10 hours painting. She uses $\frac{3}{4}$ gallon of paint every hour. How many gallons of paint does she use?

2. Dwayne has a board that is $\frac{8}{9}$ yard long. He needs to cut the board into four equal pieces. How long will each piece be?

3. Dalia has 3 pounds of butter. One batch of cookies uses $\frac{1}{2}$ pound of butter. How many batches of cookies can she make with 3 pounds of butter?

4. The doctor takes $\frac{3}{4}$ hour to complete each appointment. How long would it take the doctor to complete 12 appointments?

5. Josie has $\frac{3}{4}$ gallon of milk. She needs to divide it equally among six small bottles. How much milk will she place in each bottle?

▶ 8.8 Dividing Mixed Numbers   Exercise 72

Remember to change mixed numbers to improper fractions before dividing.

Divide. $3\frac{2}{5} \div \frac{3}{10}$ $\frac{17}{5} \div \frac{3}{10}$

$$\frac{17}{\cancel{5}_{1}} \times \frac{\cancel{10}^{2}}{3} = \frac{34}{3} = 11\frac{1}{3}$$

Divide. Remember to change the mixed numbers to fractions.

1. $3\frac{1}{2} \div \frac{1}{2} =$ **2.** $4\frac{1}{5} \div \frac{3}{10} =$ **3.** $\frac{3}{4} \div 1\frac{1}{3} =$ **4.** $2\frac{2}{3} \div 12 =$

5. $3\frac{3}{8} \div \frac{9}{10} =$ **6.** $7\frac{1}{8} \div \frac{1}{4} =$ **7.** $2\frac{2}{5} \div \frac{4}{5} =$ **8.** $\frac{4}{9} \div 2\frac{1}{4} =$

9. $\frac{7}{12} \div 2\frac{1}{4} =$ **10.** $5\frac{1}{4} \div \frac{9}{16} =$ **11.** $\frac{4}{5} \div 1\frac{1}{2} =$ **12.** $2\frac{3}{4} \div \frac{9}{10} =$

CRITICAL THINKING

Solve the problem. Show your work.

1. Students take turns helping in the front office in $\frac{1}{2}$-hour shifts. How many $\frac{1}{2}$-hour shifts are there in $9\frac{1}{2}$ hours?

2. To stay on schedule, the members of the biking club want to cover 50 miles in $2\frac{1}{2}$ hours. How many miles should they cover in 1 hour?

▶ 8.9 Duplicate Dividing Mixed Numbers by Mixed Numbers

Remember to change mixed numbers to improper fractions before dividing.

Divide. $\quad 3\frac{3}{5} \div 2\frac{1}{4} \qquad\qquad \frac{18}{5} \div \frac{9}{4}$

$$\frac{\overset{2}{\cancel{18}}}{5} \times \frac{4}{\underset{1}{\cancel{9}}} = \frac{8}{5} = 1\frac{3}{5}$$

Divide. Remember to change mixed numbers to improper fractions.

1. $2\frac{1}{2} \div 1\frac{1}{3} =$ **2.** $4\frac{1}{8} \div 1\frac{1}{4} =$ **3.** $5\frac{3}{7} \div \frac{2}{7} =$ **4.** $4\frac{5}{7} \div 4\frac{5}{7} =$

5. $12 \div 3\frac{1}{2} =$ **6.** $4\frac{3}{4} \div 2\frac{3}{8} =$ **7.** $6\frac{3}{4} \div 3\frac{3}{8} =$ **8.** $4\frac{1}{2} \div 2 =$

9. $2\frac{2}{7} \div 4 =$ **10.** $3\frac{3}{5} \div 2\frac{1}{4} =$ **11.** $3\frac{3}{4} \div 1\frac{2}{7} =$ **12.** $4\frac{3}{9} \div \frac{13}{15} =$

CRITICAL THINKING

Solve each problem. Show your work.

1. Neil hiked $5\frac{1}{4}$ miles in 3 hours. How far did he hike in 1 hour?

2. Sami bought $1\frac{1}{2}$ yards of material to make two shirts. Each shirt used the same amount of fabric. How much fabric is needed to make one shirt?

8.10 Problem Solving: Does the Answer Make Sense?

Remember to check your answer to a word problem to see if it makes sense.

The outer wall of a house is $\frac{3}{4}$ foot thick. $\frac{1}{2}$ of this wall is insulation. How thick is the insulation of the house?

PLAN   Look for a clue word.
The word *of* means to multiply. $\frac{1}{2}$ of $\frac{3}{4}$ = ?

DO   Multiply. $\frac{1}{2} \times \frac{3}{4} = \frac{3}{8}$

CHECK   Is the answer less than $\frac{3}{4}$? $\frac{3}{4} = \frac{6}{8}$ $\frac{3}{8} < \frac{6}{8}$ ✓

The insulation is $\frac{3}{8}$ foot thick.

READ the problem. Make a PLAN. DO the plan to solve the problem. CHECK your answer to see if it makes sense.

1. How many pieces of fabric that are $2\frac{1}{2}$ feet long can be cut from a 20-foot piece of fabric?

2. A recipe calls for $2\frac{2}{3}$ cups of flour. Jay wants to make $\frac{1}{2}$ of the recipe. How much flour should Jay use?

3. A bakery has $12\frac{1}{2}$ pounds of flour that it wants to divide into four equal bags. How many pounds of flour will go into each bag?

4. Marty's goal over the summer was to save $400. So far, he has saved $\frac{4}{5}$ of his goal. How much has he saved so far?

5. The stock price of Yip Co. was $8. The next day it was $2\frac{1}{4}$ times that price. What was the new price?

▶ 9.1 Adding and Subtracting Like Fractions

Remember to write the answer in lowest terms.

Add. $\quad \dfrac{11}{12} + \dfrac{5}{12}$

$$\begin{aligned} &\frac{11}{12}\\ +&\frac{5}{12}\\ \hline &\frac{16}{12} = 1\frac{4}{12} = 1\frac{1}{3} \end{aligned}$$

Subtract. $\quad \dfrac{7}{9} - \dfrac{4}{9}$

$$\begin{aligned} &\frac{7}{9}\\ -&\frac{4}{9}\\ \hline &\frac{3}{9} = \frac{1}{3} \end{aligned}$$

Add. Write the answers in lowest terms.

1. $\quad \dfrac{1}{5}$
$+\dfrac{2}{5}$

2. $\quad \dfrac{4}{7}$
$+\dfrac{2}{7}$

3. $\quad \dfrac{3}{4}$
$+\dfrac{3}{4}$

4. $\quad \dfrac{5}{6}$
$+\dfrac{5}{6}$

5. $\dfrac{5}{12} + \dfrac{7}{12} =$

6. $\dfrac{3}{10} + \dfrac{7}{10} =$

7. $\dfrac{5}{12} + \dfrac{5}{12} =$

Subtract. Write the answer in lowest terms.

8. $\quad \dfrac{9}{10}$
$-\dfrac{3}{10}$

9. $\quad \dfrac{9}{16}$
$-\dfrac{3}{16}$

10. $\quad \dfrac{5}{9}$
$-\dfrac{2}{9}$

11. $\quad \dfrac{7}{8}$
$-\dfrac{3}{8}$

12. $\dfrac{7}{8} - \dfrac{1}{8} =$

13. $\dfrac{9}{13} - \dfrac{7}{13} =$

14. $\dfrac{5}{8} - \dfrac{1}{8} =$

CRITICAL THINKING

Solve the problem. Show your work.

Walter drank $\dfrac{1}{4}$ gallon of milk yesterday and $\dfrac{1}{4}$ gallon of milk today. How much milk did he drink during these 2 days?

◣ 9.2 Adding Like Mixed Numbers **Exercise 76**

Add the fractions. Then add the whole numbers.

Add. $2\frac{2}{7} + 6\frac{6}{7}$

$$2\frac{2}{7}$$
$$+ 6\frac{6}{7}$$
$$8\frac{8}{7} = 8 + 1\frac{1}{7} = 9\frac{1}{7}$$

Add. Write the answer in lowest terms.

1. $\quad 7\frac{3}{8}$
$\quad + 5\frac{3}{8}$

2. $\quad 3\frac{5}{7}$
$\quad + 8\frac{3}{7}$

3. $\quad 4\frac{3}{11}$
$\quad + 2\frac{8}{11}$

4. $\quad 4\frac{3}{4}$
$\quad + 3$

5. $\quad 2\frac{9}{10}$
$\quad + 5\frac{7}{10}$

6. $\quad 6\frac{7}{12}$
$\quad + 5\frac{11}{12}$

7. $\quad 5\frac{5}{6}$
$\quad + 9\frac{5}{6}$

8. $\quad 8\frac{5}{8}$
$\quad + \frac{7}{8}$

9. $9\frac{3}{7} + 8\frac{2}{7} =$

10. $7\frac{5}{13} + 9\frac{9}{13} =$

11. $8\frac{9}{14} + 5\frac{5}{14} =$

12. $6\frac{7}{15} + 7 =$

CRITICAL THINKING

Solve the problem. Show your work.

Annabel read her book for $\frac{4}{5}$ hour in the morning. She then read for $1\frac{3}{5}$ hours in the afternoon. How much time did she spend reading during the day?

▶ 9.3 Subtracting Like Mixed Numbers   Exercise 77

Regroup when the top numerator is smaller than the bottom numerator.

Subtract. $11\frac{3}{10} - 5\frac{1}{10}$ Subtract. $11\frac{1}{10} - 5\frac{3}{10}$

$$
\begin{array}{r}
11\frac{3}{10} \\
-\ 5\frac{1}{10} \\
\hline
6\frac{2}{10} = 6\frac{1}{5}
\end{array}
$$

$$
\begin{array}{r}
11\frac{1}{10} = \quad 10\frac{11}{10} \\
-\ 5\frac{3}{10} = -\ 5\frac{3}{10} \\
\hline
5\frac{8}{10} = 5\frac{4}{5}
\end{array}
$$

Subtract. Regroup, if necessary.

1. $\quad 7\frac{3}{8}$
    $-\ 5\frac{1}{8}$

2. $\quad 8\frac{2}{3}$
    $-\ 3\frac{1}{3}$

3. $\quad 16\frac{9}{14}$
    $-\ 2\frac{7}{14}$

4. $\quad 12\frac{3}{10}$
    $-\ 8\frac{7}{10}$

5. $\quad 5\frac{4}{9}$
    $-\ 3\frac{5}{9}$

6. $\quad 7\frac{7}{10}$
    $-\ 2\frac{9}{10}$

7. $\quad 14\frac{7}{15}$
    $-\ 3\frac{11}{15}$

8. $\quad 6\frac{7}{12}$
    $-\ 4\frac{11}{12}$

9. $\quad 9\frac{1}{4}$
    $-\ 4\frac{3}{4}$

10. $\quad 8\frac{17}{20}$
    $-\ 2\frac{13}{20}$

11. $\quad 6\frac{11}{18}$
    $-\ 2\frac{13}{18}$

12. $\quad 8\frac{7}{16}$
    $-\ 4\frac{9}{16}$

CRITICAL THINKING

Solve the problem. Show your work.

In all, Earl spent $1\frac{1}{6}$ hours studying math and world history. Of this, he spent $\frac{5}{6}$ hour studying world history. What part of an hour did he spend studying math? How many minutes did he spend studying math?

▶ 9.4 Subtracting from a Whole Number   Exercise 78

Regroup the whole number as a mixed number.

Subtract. $5 - 2\frac{1}{4}$

$$5 = 4\frac{4}{4}$$
$$-2\frac{1}{4} = -2\frac{1}{4}$$
$$\overline{\hspace{1cm}2\frac{3}{4}}$$

Subtract. Remember to regroup the whole number.

1. 7
   $-3\frac{5}{8}$

2. 9
   $-6\frac{3}{10}$

3. 6
   $-3\frac{1}{2}$

4. 8
   $-5\frac{1}{9}$

5. 3
   $-2\frac{4}{7}$

6. 12
   $-4\frac{7}{15}$

7. 15
   $-7\frac{5}{12}$

8. 13
   $-9\frac{8}{11}$

9. $5 - 3\frac{5}{8} =$

10. $18 - 7\frac{7}{12} =$

11. $50 - 35\frac{3}{20} =$

12. $37 - 24\frac{6}{15} =$

CRITICAL THINKING

Check each subtraction problem. If incorrect, show how to do the subtraction correctly.

1. $6 - 2\frac{2}{7} = 4\frac{2}{7}$

2. $8 - 2\frac{3}{8} = 6\frac{5}{8}$

3. $14 - 6\frac{4}{9} = 6\frac{5}{9}$

▶ 9.5 Adding Unlike Fractions   Exercise 79

Make like fractions. Use a common denominator.

Add. $\frac{2}{5} + \frac{3}{4}$

$$\frac{2}{5} = \frac{2 \times 4}{5 \times 4} = \frac{8}{20}$$

$$+ \frac{3}{4} = \frac{3 \times 5}{4 \times 5} = + \frac{15}{20}$$

$$\frac{23}{20} = 1\frac{3}{20}$$

Add. Remember to rename as like fractions.

1. $\frac{1}{6}$
       $+ \frac{1}{3}$

2. $\frac{3}{4}$
       $+ \frac{1}{6}$

3. $\frac{3}{5}$
       $+ \frac{4}{10}$

4. $\frac{5}{6}$
       $+ \frac{4}{9}$

5. $\frac{1}{2}$
       $+ \frac{3}{4}$

6. $\frac{7}{8}$
       $+ \frac{3}{4}$

7. $\frac{8}{9}$
       $+ \frac{1}{3}$

8. $\frac{2}{3}$
       $+ \frac{1}{12}$

9. $\frac{3}{5} + \frac{5}{6} =$

10. $\frac{5}{6} + \frac{7}{12} =$

11. $\frac{1}{2} + \frac{2}{3} =$

12. $\frac{2}{3} + \frac{1}{5} =$

CRITICAL THINKING

Alan got two questions wrong on his math quiz. Do the addition and find his errors.

1. $\frac{13}{20}$
       $+ \frac{4}{5}$
       $\overline{\frac{17}{20}}$

2. $\frac{4}{7}$
       $+ \frac{4}{21}$
       $\overline{\frac{8}{28}}$

9.6 Subtracting Unlike Fractions   Exercise 80

Make like fractions. Use a common denominator.

Subtract. $\dfrac{5}{6} - \dfrac{3}{8}$

$$\dfrac{5}{6} = \dfrac{5 \times 4}{6 \times 4} = \dfrac{20}{24}$$

$$-\dfrac{3}{8} = \dfrac{3 \times 3}{8 \times 3} = -\dfrac{9}{24}$$

$$\dfrac{11}{24}$$

Subtract. Remember to rename as like fractions.

1. $\dfrac{2}{3}$ $-\dfrac{1}{4}$

2. $\dfrac{3}{5}$ $-\dfrac{1}{2}$

3. $\dfrac{2}{3}$ $-\dfrac{1}{6}$

4. $\dfrac{1}{2}$ $-\dfrac{3}{10}$

5. $\dfrac{5}{6}$ $-\dfrac{3}{4}$

6. $\dfrac{7}{10}$ $-\dfrac{1}{2}$

7. $\dfrac{9}{10}$ $-\dfrac{7}{15}$

8. $\dfrac{8}{9}$ $-\dfrac{2}{3}$

9. $\dfrac{1}{2} - \dfrac{2}{5} =$

10. $\dfrac{7}{8} - \dfrac{2}{3} =$

11. $\dfrac{7}{8} - \dfrac{1}{2} =$

12. $\dfrac{3}{4} - \dfrac{7}{16} =$

CRITICAL THINKING

Fill in the missing numbers.

1. $\dfrac{2}{3}$ $-\dfrac{\blacksquare}{\blacksquare}$ $\dfrac{1}{6}$

2. $\dfrac{\blacksquare}{\blacksquare}$ $-\dfrac{1}{2}$ $\dfrac{3}{8}$

3. $\dfrac{23}{25}$ $-\dfrac{\blacksquare}{\blacksquare}$ 0

▶ 9.7 Adding Unlike Mixed Numbers   Exercise 81

Make like mixed numbers. Use a common denominator.

Add.　　$8\frac{2}{3} + 5\frac{1}{2}$　　　　$8\frac{2}{3} = \quad 8\frac{4}{6}$

$\qquad\qquad\qquad\qquad\quad + 5\frac{1}{2} = + 5\frac{3}{6}$

$\qquad\qquad\qquad\qquad\qquad\quad 13\frac{7}{6} = 13 + 1\frac{1}{6} = 14\frac{1}{6}$

Add. Remember to rename as like mixed numbers.

1.　　$3\frac{2}{5}$
　　　　$+ 1\frac{7}{20}$

2.　　$6\frac{11}{16}$
　　　　$+ 3\frac{1}{2}$

3.　　$7\frac{7}{24}$
　　　　$+ 4\frac{5}{6}$

4.　　$5\frac{1}{4}$
　　　　$+ 2\frac{5}{12}$

5.　　$1\frac{3}{4}$
　　　　$+ 1\frac{3}{10}$

6.　　$3\frac{4}{5}$
　　　　$+ 2\frac{1}{6}$

7.　　$4\frac{11}{12}$
　　　　$+ 5\frac{8}{9}$

8.　　$8\frac{5}{6}$
　　　　$+ 4\frac{7}{10}$

9.　　$3\frac{3}{4}$
　　　　$+ 4\frac{1}{3}$

10. $5\frac{7}{10} + 3\frac{7}{15} =$

11. $6\frac{3}{10} + 8\frac{5}{12} =$

12. $4\frac{5}{6} + 7\frac{3}{5} =$

13. $2\frac{1}{3} + 5\frac{1}{12} =$

CRITICAL THINKING

Solve the problem. Show your work.

Dena needs $2\frac{1}{2}$ cups of flour to make a cake and $5\frac{1}{6}$ cups of flour to make bread. How much flour does she need altogether?

▶ 9.8 Subtracting Unlike Mixed Numbers   Exercise 82

Make like mixed numbers. Use a common denominator. Sometimes, you may need to regroup the first mixed number to subtract.

Subtract. $4\frac{3}{4} - 2\frac{2}{3}$

$$4\frac{3}{4} = 4\frac{9}{12}$$
$$-\,2\frac{2}{3} = -\,2\frac{8}{12}$$
$$\overline{\qquad 2\frac{1}{12}}$$

Subtract. $4\frac{2}{3} - 2\frac{3}{4}$

$$4\frac{2}{3} = 4\frac{8}{12} = 3\frac{20}{12}$$
$$-\,2\frac{3}{4} = -\,2\frac{9}{12} = -\,2\frac{9}{12}$$
$$\overline{\qquad\qquad\qquad 1\frac{11}{12}}$$

Subtract. Regroup, if necessary.

1. $8\frac{7}{12}$
   $-\,5\frac{5}{6}$

2. $14\frac{2}{5}$
   $-\,7\frac{9}{10}$

3. $5\frac{4}{9}$
   $-\,3\frac{1}{6}$

4. $3\frac{4}{5}$
   $-\,1\frac{1}{2}$

5. $5\frac{2}{3}$
   $-\,3\frac{4}{9}$

6. $6\frac{3}{8}$
   $-\,2\frac{1}{2}$

7. $5\frac{1}{6}$
   $-\,2\frac{5}{8}$

8. $3\frac{3}{8}$
   $-\,2\frac{7}{10}$

9. $6\frac{8}{9}$
   $-\,1\frac{1}{2}$

10. $14\frac{2}{5} - 3\frac{11}{15} =$

11. $16\frac{9}{14} - 12\frac{3}{7} =$

12. $24\frac{7}{20} - 10\frac{3}{10} =$

13. $5\frac{2}{3} - 1\frac{1}{5} =$

CRITICAL THINKING

Solve the problem. Show your work.

Teresa had $29\frac{5}{8}$ yards of fabric. On Friday, she used $26\frac{1}{2}$ yards of the fabric. How much fabric does she have left?

◤ 9.9 Problem Solving: Multi-Part Problems

Exercise 83

To solve multi-part problems, work on one part at a time.

Ida used 3 quarts of pineapple juice and $2\frac{1}{4}$ quarts of orange juice to make punch. Her guests drank $1\frac{1}{2}$ quarts of the punch. How much punch was left?

PLAN Add to find the total punch made.
Subtract to find the amount of punch that is left.

DO Add.

$$
\begin{array}{r}
3 \text{ quarts} \\
+\ 2\frac{1}{4} \text{ quarts} \\
\hline
5\frac{1}{4} \text{ quarts}
\end{array}
$$

Subtract.

$$
\begin{array}{r}
5\frac{1}{4} \text{ quarts} \\
-\ 1\frac{1}{2} \text{ quarts} \\
\hline
3\frac{3}{4} \text{ quarts}
\end{array}
$$

Ida had $3\frac{3}{4}$ quarts of punch left.

READ the problem. Make a PLAN. DO the plan to solve the problem.

1. Frank had $1\frac{3}{8}$ packages of dog treats. He bought 2 more packages. His dog ate $3\frac{1}{4}$ packages. How many packages were left over?

2. Celia had $11\frac{1}{3}$ yards of rope. She used $6\frac{1}{4}$ yards of rope to mark off the shallow area of the community pool. She used $2\frac{1}{2}$ yards to mark off the diving area. How much rope was left?

3. Justin made his costume for the play. He needed $2\frac{2}{5}$ yards for the shirt and $3\frac{3}{5}$ yards for the pants. Each yard cost $5. What is his total cost?

4. Irene bought 5 gallons of paint. She used $2\frac{1}{2}$ gallons of paint for her kitchen and $1\frac{3}{4}$ gallons of paint for her bedroom. How much paint was left?

5. Tara had 20 cups of flour. She wanted to bake three loaves of bread and needed $5\frac{1}{4}$ cups of flour for each loaf. How much flour was left?

Name_____   Date_____

A decimal is a number that names part of a whole.

Tenths   Hundredths   Ones   Tenths

   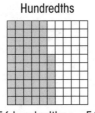   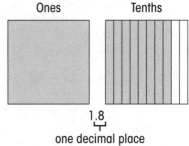

3 tenths = .3   56 hundredths = .56   1.8
one decimal place   two decimal places   one decimal place

The decimal places are to the right of the decimal point.

Shade each square to show the decimal.

1.   Tenths   **2.**   Hundredths   **3.**   Ones   Tenths

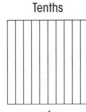   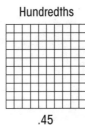   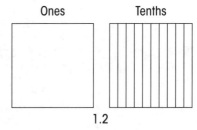

.6   .45   1.2

Draw a line under each decimal part. Then, tell the number of decimal places.

4. 16.01   **5.** 18.7093   **6.** .805   **7.** 25

8. 5.222   **9.** 400   **10.** 7.00   **11.** 9.1

CRITICAL THINKING

Shade the square.

This square has been shaded to show the
decimal .60. Darken $\frac{1}{2}$ of the shaded boxes.
What decimal do the darkened boxes show?

Hundredths

Name _____ Date _____

The place-value chart can help you to read and write decimals.

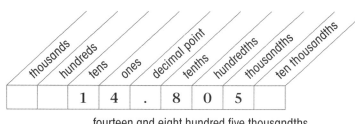

fourteen and eight hundred five thousandths

Write each decimal in words.

1. 23.456 _____

2. 9.067 _____

3. .53 _____

Write each number as a decimal.

4. six hundred fifty-four and seventy-six hundredths _____

5. four hundred eighty-five thousandths _____

6. twelve and six thousandths _____

7. nine and eight hundred twenty-three thousandths _____

CRITICAL THINKING

The average rainfall for two cities are listed. Write each decimal in words.

1. Phoenix, 7.66 inches _____

2. Chicago, 35.82 inches _____

Name _____ Date _____

▶ 10.3 Comparing Decimals   Exercise 86

> When you compare decimals, first compare the whole number parts. Then compare the decimal parts.
>
> Compare.   25.96 and 25.9
>
> Whole number parts are the same.   25.96   25.9
>
> Add one zero. Compare the decimal parts.   25.96   25.90
>
>   25.96 > 25.9

Compare each pair of numbers. Use <, >, or =.

1. 8.59 _____ 9.32   **2.** 25.85 _____ 28.87   **3.** 56.28 _____ 28.97

4. .235 _____ .951   **5.** 357.1 _____ 356.8   **6.** 4.56 _____ 1.23

7. .951 _____ .742   **8.** 865.42 _____ 865.32   **9.** 65 _____ 6.24

10. 58.256 _____ 58.27   **11.** 36.27 _____ 36.2   **12.** 75.32 _____ 75.02

13. 25.96 _____ 26.8   **14.** 60 _____ 59.9   **15.** 541.25 _____ 540.45

CRITICAL THINKING

Which baseball player had the better batting average? Underline the correct one in each problem.

1. Daryl Strawberry at .262   or   Mark McGwire at .304

2. Cal Ripken at .278   or   Danny Goodwin at .292

3. Tony Gwynn at .353   or   Don Mueller at .330

▶ 10.4 Ordering Decimals   Exercise 87

> Write these decimals in order from greatest to least.   8.6   8.034   8.19
>
>   Write zeros so that all the decimals have the same number of decimal places.
>
>   8.600 ← greatest
>
> The whole numbers are the same.   8.034 ← least
>
> Compare the decimal parts.   8.190 ← middle
>
> The decimals in order from largest to smallest are: 8.6   8.19   8.034

Write the decimals in order from greatest to least.

1. .356   .257   1.89

2. 96.58   657.8   .87

3. 65.4   65.8   28.95

4. .851   .659   1.486

5. 3.86   3.07   3.93

6. 45.8   45   45.08

CRITICAL THINKING

Oakland and San Francisco played each other in a World Series. Put each team's players in order from best to worst using their batting averages.

Oakland		San Francisco	
T. Steinbach	.250	K. Mitchell	.294
D. Henderson	.308	W. Clark	.250
R. Henderson	.474	M. Williams	.125
T. Phillips	.235	B. Butler	.286

◤ 10.5 Adding Decimals   Exercise 88

> When you add decimals, you need to line up the decimal points.
> Remember to write zeros, if needed.
>
> Add.   7 + .139 + 8.9
>
> $$\begin{array}{r} 1 \\ 7.000 \\ .139 \\ +\ 8.900 \\ \hline 16.039 \end{array}$$

Add. The decimal points have been lined up for you.

1.   9.37
   + 6.44

2.   8.49
   + 2.53

3. $5.47
   +   .93

4. $8.06
   + 3.98

5.   17.35
   + 9.81

6.   49.08
   + 51.73

7. $164.29
   +   46.15

8. $295.50
   +   38.05

Add. Be sure to line up the decimal points.

9. 16 + 133.27 =

10. 175.8 + 54.72 =

11. 69 + 7.52 =

12. 17.9 + 5.436 =

13. 41.85 + 2.909 + 8 =

14. $50 + $28.07 + $5.78 =

15. 16.39 + 9.2 + .515 =

16. $68.36 + $102 + $1.98 =

CRITICAL THINKING

Find the missing numbers. Tell how you found each missing number.

1. $2,900.84 + ▮▮▮▮▮ = $3,000.90

2. ▮▮▮▮▮ + 300.80 = $1,000.00

▶ 10.6 Subtracting Decimals   **Exercise 89**

When you subtract decimals, you need to line up the decimal points. Remember to write zeros, if needed.

Subtract.   83.89 − 4.8   Subtract.   65 − 6.257

$$
\begin{array}{r}
83.89 \\
-\ 4.80 \\
\hline
79.09
\end{array}
$$

$$
\begin{array}{r}
\overset{14}{} \\
5\!\!\!/\ 9\,9\,10 \\
6\!\!\!/5.000 \\
-\ 6.257 \\
\hline
58.743
\end{array}
$$

Subtract. The decimal points have been lined up for you.

1. $\begin{array}{r} 3.058 \\ -\ 2.890 \\ \hline \end{array}$ **2.** $\begin{array}{r} 25.98 \\ -\ 7.28 \\ \hline \end{array}$ **3.** $\begin{array}{r} \$8.98 \\ -\ 6.65 \\ \hline \end{array}$ **4.** $\begin{array}{r} \$57.26 \\ -\ 25.84 \\ \hline \end{array}$

5. $\begin{array}{r} 98.54 \\ -\ 56.80 \\ \hline \end{array}$ **6.** $\begin{array}{r} 54.08 \\ -\ 6.97 \\ \hline \end{array}$ **7.** $\begin{array}{r} \$157.35 \\ -\ 35.87 \\ \hline \end{array}$ **8.** $\begin{array}{r} \$85.24 \\ -\ 4.08 \\ \hline \end{array}$

Subtract. Be sure to line up the decimal points.

9. $87 - 23.06 =$ **10.** $851.6 - 48.03 =$

11. $55.28 - 6.024 =$ **12.** $74.563 - 6.789 =$

13. $\$6.25 - \$6 =$ **14.** $\$8 - \$5.05 =$

15. $\$850 - \$24.89 =$ **16.** $\$145.96 - \$56.96 =$

CRITICAL THINKING

Subtract. Show your work.

1. $6 - .8 =$ **2.** $6 - .5 =$ **3.** $6 - .3 =$ **4.** $6 - .2 =$

5. After doing the previous exercises, what do you think $6 - .7$ would be?

▶ 10.7 Multiplying Decimals   Exercise 90

Add the number of decimal places in the factors to find the number of decimal places in the product.

Multiply. $4.3 \times .02$

$$\begin{array}{r} 4.3 \\ \times\ .02 \\ \hline .086 \end{array}$$ 1 decimal place
2 decimal places
← 3 decimal places

↑
Write a zero.

Multiply.

1.   2.08
      $\times\ .03$

2.   5.69
      $\times\ 1.7$

3. $23.50
      $\times\ 2.4$

4. $152.35
      $\times\ .62$

5.   .468
      $\times\ .01$

6.   9.37
      $\times\ 5.9$

7. $70.83
      $\times\ 3.8$

8.   3.97
      $\times\ .75$

9. $9.8 \times .06 =$

10. $.975 \times 10.8 =$

11. $63.20 \times .74 =$

12. $58.4 \times 60 =$

13. $36 \times .195 =$

14. $.007 \times .8 =$

CRITICAL THINKING

Find each product. Write the words that describe the pattern.

1. $652 \times 5 =$

2. $652 \times .5 =$

3. $652 \times .05 =$

4. As one factor becomes _____ (smaller, larger),

the product becomes _____ (smaller, larger).

▶ 10.8 Multiplying Decimals by 10, 100, 1,000   Exercise 91

> When you multiply by 10, by 100, and by 1,000, you move the decimal point to the right. Write zeros if needed.
>
> | 1 zero, move 1 place | 2 zeros, move 2 places | 3 zeros, move 3 places |
> |---|---|---|
> | $.058 \times 10 = 0.58 = .58$ | $.058 \times 100 = 05.8 = 5.8$ | $.058 \times 1,000 = 058 = 58$ |

Find each product.

1. $25.4 \times 10 =$

2. $3.5 \times 10 =$

3. $8.93 \times 10 =$

4. $.76 \times 10 =$

5. $.234 \times 100 =$

6. $75.67 \times 100 =$

7. $6.567 \times 100 =$

8. $846.7 \times 100 =$

9. $33.45 \times 1,000 =$

10. $.457 \times 1,000 =$

11. $8.903 \times 1,000 =$

12. $3.46 \times 1,000 =$

13. $53.35 \times 10 =$

14. $77.87 \times 100 =$

15. $.789 \times 1,000 =$

CRITICAL THINKING

Multiply.

1. $138 \times .1 =$

2. $138 \times .01 =$

3. $138 \times .001 =$

4. $138 \times .0001 =$

5. After doing the previous exercises, what do you think $138 \times .00001$ would be?

Name_____ Date_____

▶ 10.9 Dividing Decimals by Whole Numbers   Exercise 92

Place the decimal points in the quotient above the decimal in the dividend. If the decimal quotient has a repeating pattern, draw a bar over this pattern.

Divide.

$$
\begin{array}{r}
.061 \\
6\overline{)\,.366} \\
36 \\
\hline
06 \\
6 \\
\hline
0
\end{array}
$$

$$
.02121 \rightarrow .0\overline{21}
$$
$$
\begin{array}{r}
66\overline{)\,1.40000} \\
132 \\
\hline
80 \\
66 \\
\hline
140 \\
132 \\
\hline
80 \\
66 \\
\hline
14
\end{array}
$$

Divide. Place the decimal point in the quotient. Write zeros if needed.

1. $7\overline{)24.5}$ **2.** $8\overline{).336}$ **3.** $21\overline{)69.3}$

4. $83\overline{)63.08}$ **5.** $4\overline{)24.4}$ **6.** $37\overline{)1.739}$

Divide. Draw a bar over the repeating part of the quotient.

7. $11\overline{)3.6}$ **8.** $33\overline{)6.9}$ **9.** $22\overline{)5.8}$

CRITICAL THINKING

Solve each problem. Show your work.

1. A wire .8 inch long is to be cut into 4 pieces. If each piece is the same length, how long will each piece be?

2. Each of 7 dogs has the same weight. Their total weight is 42.42 pounds. How much does each dog weigh?

► 10.10 Dividing Decimals by Decimals   **Exercise 93**

When you divide decimals, move the decimal points so that the divisor becomes a whole number. Add zeros to the dividend if needed.

Divide. $4.5\overline{)21.54}$ = $4.7866 \rightarrow 4.78\overline{6}$

$$45.\overline{)215.4000}$$

$$
\begin{array}{r}
-\ 180 \\
\hline
354 \\
-\ 315 \\
\hline
390 \\
-\ 360 \\
\hline
300 \\
-\ 270 \\
\hline
300 \\
-\ 270 \\
\hline
30
\end{array}
$$

Divide.

1. $.3\overline{)6}$

2. $.6\overline{).72}$

3. $.7\overline{)35.7}$

4. $.6\overline{)55.2}$

5. $.04\overline{).068}$

6. $.07\overline{)2.52}$

7. $.15\overline{)18}$

8. $.73\overline{)5.986}$

9. $.11\overline{).68}$

10. $.22\overline{).42}$

11. $.44\overline{).632}$

12. $.50\overline{)7.5}$

CRITICAL THINKING

Find the quotient. Write the words that describe the pattern.

1. $2\overline{)38}$

2. $.2\overline{)38}$

3. $.02\overline{)38}$

4. As the divisor becomes _____ (smaller, larger),

the quotient becomes _____ (smaller, larger).

▶ 10.11 Dividing Decimals by 10, 100, 1,000   Exercise 94

When you divide by 10, by 100, and by 1,000, you move
the decimal point to the left. Write zeros if needed.

1 zero, move 1 place	2 zeros, move 2 places	3 zeros, move 3 places
$96 \div 10 = 9.6$	$96 \div 100 = .96$	$96 \div 1{,}000 = .096$

Find each quotient.

1. $65.4 \div 10 =$ **2.** $872.45 \div 10 =$ **3.** $35.49 \div 10 =$

4. $54.3 \div 10 =$ **5.** $24.3 \div 100 =$ **6.** $587.2 \div 100 =$

7. $2.54 \div 100 =$ **8.** $742.36 \div 100 =$ **9.** $65.42 \div 1{,}000 =$

10. $.25 \div 1{,}000 =$ **11.** $987 \div 1{,}000 =$ **12.** $45.67 \div 1{,}000 =$

13. $9.07 \div 100 =$ **14.** $84.67 \div 10 =$ **15.** $.687 \div 1{,}000 =$

CRITICAL THINKING

Divide.

1. $138 \div .1 =$ **2.** $138 \div .01 =$ **3.** $138 \div .001 =$ **4.** $138 \div .0001 =$

5. After doing the previous exercises, what do you think $138 \div .00001$ would be?

10.12 Problem Solving: Multi-Part Problems

To solve multi-part problems, work on one part at a time.

Mike bought juice that costs $1.79. He also bought milk that costs $2.39. Mike had a 25¢ coupon. How much change from $5 did he receive?

PLAN Add purchases   Subtract coupon   Subtract total cost

DO

Add purchases	Subtract coupon	Subtract total cost
$1.79 Juice	$4.18	$5.00
+ 2.39 Milk	− .25 Coupon	− 3.93
$4.18	$3.93 Total cost	$1.07 Change

Solve each problem.

1. Sam bought $\frac{1}{2}$ pound of cheese. The cheese costs $3.58 a pound. He also bought three energy bars. Each energy bar costs $1.25. What was the total cost?

2. Toothpaste costs $2.69. Dental floss costs $1.29. Soap costs $.49 a bar. Elvin bought one of each item. He had $10 and a 50¢ coupon for the toothpaste. How much does he have left?

3. Jana won $100 in a contest. She decided to spend some of the money on a new camera. She put the rest in savings. She bought the camera for $49.00, three packs of film for $4.39 each, and a camera case for $19.98. How much did she put in savings?

4. Justin wanted to buy five notebooks for $2.89 each, a protractor for $3.25, and a mechanical pencil for $3.50. He had $20. How much more did he need?

5. Pens cost $3.75 for three. Pencils are $2.50 a dozen. Paper is $4.39 a box. Marie bought one pen, a dozen pencils, and a box of paper. What was the total cost?

▶ 10.13 Renaming Decimals as Fractions   Exercise 96

> To rename decimals as fractions, use the decimal digits as the numerator and the last place value as the denominator.
>
> Rename the decimal .36 as a fraction in lowest terms.
>
> $$.36 = 36 \text{ hundredths} = \frac{36}{100} = \frac{36 \div 4}{100 \div 4} = \frac{9}{25}$$

Rename each decimal as a fraction. Reduce the fraction to lowest terms.

1. .5   **2.** .25   **3.** .875   **4.** .9

5. .84   **6.** .455   **7.** .8   **8.** .98

9. .375   **10.** .4   **11.** .65   **12.** .625

13. .3   **14.** .08   **15.** .004   **16.** .014

CRITICAL THINKING

Solve each problem. Show your work.

1. $.50 is what fraction of a dollar? Reduce the fraction to lowest terms.

2. If Sue's batting average is .250, what fraction of her times at bat does she get a hit?

▶ 10.14 Renaming Fractions as Decimals   Exercise 97

To rename fractions as decimals, divide the numerator by the denominator.

Rename the fraction $\frac{8}{50}$ as a decimal.

$$\frac{8}{50} = 50\overline{)8.00} \quad \begin{array}{r} .16 \\ \hline -5\,0 \\ \hline 300 \\ -300 \\ \hline 0 \end{array}$$

Rename each fraction as a decimal by using division.

1. $\frac{3}{5}$

2. $\frac{7}{20}$

3. $\frac{19}{50}$

4. $\frac{3}{4}$

5. $\frac{1}{2}$

6. $\frac{9}{250}$

7. $\frac{17}{500}$

8. $\frac{8}{20}$

9. $\frac{9}{20}$

10. $\frac{3}{125}$

11. $\frac{19}{40}$

12. $\frac{2}{5}$

13. $\frac{23}{100}$

14. $\frac{5}{8}$

15. $\frac{47}{200}$

16. $\frac{1}{4}$

CRITICAL THINKING

The average wind speed in miles per hour for three cities during one year is listed in the chart to the right. Change the numbers from fractions to decimals.

City	Average Wind Speed
Albuquerque, NM	$8\frac{9}{10}$
Milwaukee, WI	$11\frac{1}{2}$
New Orleans, LA	$8\frac{1}{5}$

Name _____ Date _____

Round the decimal 5.683 to the nearest hundredth.

Underline the rounding place.	5.6<u>8</u>3
Look at the digit to its right.	↑
Compare the digit to 5.	3 is smaller than 5
Round as you would whole numbers.	Leave 8.
Drop all digits to the right of the rounding place.	5.68

The decimal 5.683 rounded to the nearest hundredth is 5.68.

Round each decimal to the nearest tenth.

1. 5.87   **2.** 45.92   **3.** 763.24   **4.** 84.65

5. 98.73   **6.** 8.57   **7.** 47.52   **8.** 30.97

Round each decimal to the nearest hundredth or cent.

9. 6.852   **10.** $74.128   **11.** $60.123   **12.** 85.049

13. 5.245   **14.** 98.996   **15.** 8.025   **16.** 7.954

CRITICAL THINKING

List 3 possible numbers that will round to the nearest tenth and become:

1. 9.4   **2.** 10.1

Name _____ Date _____

A percent is part of a whole that is divided into 100 equal parts.
The sign for percent is %.

35%

A percent more than 100% is more than one whole.

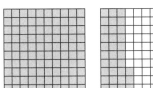

133%

Write the percent for the part shaded in each model.

1.

2.

3.

4.

5.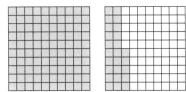

6.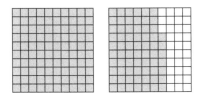

CRITICAL THINKING

John read 65% of his book. Hannah read 75% of her book.
Each student read the same book. Who read the least?

▶ 11.2 Changing Percents to Decimals

> To change a percent to a decimal, move the decimal point
> two places to the left.
>
> $\quad$ 67% = .67 $\qquad\qquad\qquad$ 6% = .06
>
> If the percent is a mixed number, change it to a decimal first.
>
> $\quad 6\frac{1}{2}\% = 6.5\% = .065 \qquad\qquad 6\frac{3}{4}\% = 6.75\% = .0675$

Change each percent to a decimal.

1. 8% = $\qquad$ **2.** 3% = $\qquad$ **3.** 18% = $\qquad$ **4.** 46% =

5. 93% = $\qquad$ **6.** 41% = $\qquad$ **7.** 30% = $\qquad$ **8.** 40% =

9. 168% = $\qquad$ **10.** 672% = $\qquad$ **11.** 123% = $\qquad$ **12.** 60% =

13. $9\frac{3}{4}\%$ = $\qquad$ **14.** $6\frac{4}{5}\%$ = $\qquad$ **15.** 8.5% = $\qquad$ **16.** 7.75% =

CRITICAL THINKING

In Lincoln School, 75% of the teachers are women. In Hillside
School, .78 of the teachers are women. Do both schools have
the same percent of women teachers? Explain.

▶ 11.3 Finding the Part   Exercise 101

To find the part in a percent problem, multiply the percent and the whole.

What is 158% of 60?   158% = 1.58   1.58 ← Percent
       ↑   ↑ $\times$ 60 ← Whole
    Percent Whole   94.80 ← Part

Find the part.

1. 20% of 50 =

2. 65% of 98 =

3. 75% of 150 =

4. 50% of 200 =

5. 33% of 100 =

6. 25% of 300 =

Answer each question.

7. What is 65% of 85?

8. What is 82% of 200?

9. What is 42% of 135?

10. What is 55% of 159?

11. What is 99% of 202?

12. What is 77% of 120?

CRITICAL THINKING

Solve each problem. Show your work.

1. Bob's team won 75% of its baseball games.
It played 16 games in all. How many games
did the team win?

2. Last season, a basketball player scored 980 points.
He scored 40% of these points at away games.
How many points did he score at away games?

▶ 11.4 Sales Tax

> To find the sales tax, multiply the the sales tax rate by the cost of the item.
>
> A CD sells for $12.49. The sales tax is 7%. What is the amount of the sales tax? What is the total cost of the CD?
>
> | Sales tax rate | × | Cost | = | Sales tax | | Cost | + | Sales tax | = | Total cost |
> |---|---|---|---|---|---|---|---|---|---|---|
> | .07 | × | $12.49 | = | $.8743 | | $12.49 | + | $.87 | = | $13.36 |

Find the sales tax. Then find the total cost for each item.

1. A suit costs $200. The sales tax is 7%.

2. A bike costs $150. The sales tax is 5%.

3. A television sells for $179. The sales tax is 6%.

4. A CD player costs $113.40. The sales tax is 5%.

5. A notebook sells for $5.99. The sales tax is 7%.

CRITICAL THINKING

Jan bought a game for $50. The sales tax was 5%.
Bob bought a game for $48. The sales tax was 8%.
Who paid the greater total cost? How much more?

▶ 11.5 Discounts   Exercise 103

To find the discount, multiply the discount rate by the price of the item.

A coat costs $70. It is on sale at 25% off. What is the discount and the sale price?

Discount rate × Price = Discount   Original price − Discount = Sale price
   .25   × $70 = $17.50 $70   − $17.50 = $52.50

Find the discount. Then find the sale price for each item.

1. A shirt costs $32. It is on sale at 30% off.

2. A pair of jeans sells for $32. The jeans are on sale at 20% off.

3. A VCR costs $104. It is on sale at 15% off.

4. A CD costs $14.95. It is on sale at 12% off.

5. Videos are priced at $19.95. They are on sale at 10% off.

CRITICAL THINKING

Solve each problem. Show your work.

1. A watch costs $100. It is on sale at 20% off.
   After still going unsold, it goes on sale again at
   10% off the sale price. What is the final sale price?

2. A watch costs $100. It is on sale at 30% off.
   What is the sale price? Is this sale price the same as
   the final sale price in Question 1? Why or why not?

Name_____ Date_____

▶ 11.6 Commissions   Exercise 104

> To find the commission, multiply the commission rate and the total sales.
>
> Bob's base salary is $360 per week. Last week, his sales totaled $3,500. His commission is 5% of his sales. What is the amount of his commission and his gross salary for last week?
>
> | Rate | × | Sales | = | Commission | | Base salary | + | Commission | = | Gross salary |
> |------|---|-------|---|------------|---|-------------|---|------------|---|--------------|
> | .05 | × | $3,500 | = | $175 | | $360 | + | $175 | = | $535 |

Solve each problem.

1. Last week, Zachary's total sales were $5,985. His commission is 10% of his sales. What is the amount of his commission?

2. Mr. Eisenberg earns a 6% commission on his sales. His sales were $26,000. What is the amount of his commission?

3. Alicia earns a base salary of $400 per week. Her commission is 7% of her sales. If her sales last week were $2,549, what was her gross salary?

4. Last month, Justine's total sales were $3,570. She receives a 7% commission. If her base salary is $100, what was her gross salary?

5. Patty's base salary is $350 a week. Her sales this week total $1,430. If her commission is 5%, what is her gross salary?

CRITICAL THINKING

Aaron's sales are $1,500. Is it better to have a 25% commission or a base salary of $100 and 15% commission? Explain.

Name_____ Date_____

▶ 11.7 Changing Decimals to Percents   **Exercise 105**

> To change a decimal to a percent, move the decimal point
> two places to the right.
>
> $.06 = 6\%$ $.567 = 56.7\%$ $.9876 = 98.76\%$

Change each decimal to a percent.

1. .5 =   **2.** .09 =   **3.** .75 =   **4.** .67 =

5. 1.28 =   **6.** .055 =   **7.** .0875 =   **8.** .06 =

9. .3125 =   **10.** .25 =   **11.** .0095 =   **12.** .0075 =

13. 1.00 =   **14.** 7.58 =   **15.** 3.25 =   **16.** 5.14 =

17. .333 =   **18.** .7 =   **19.** .0487 =   **20.** .094 =

CRITICAL THINKING

Solve each problem. Show your work.

1. A music store sold .25 of its CDs.
   What percent of its CDs were sold?

2. Another music store sold .6 of its CDs.
   What percent of its CDs were sold?
   What percent of its CDs were not sold?

▶ 11.8 Changing Fractions to Percents   Exercise 106

To change a fraction to a percent, divide the numerator by the denominator. Then, change the decimal to a percent.

$$\frac{numerator}{denominator} \rightarrow denominator\overline{)numerator}$$

Change $\frac{1}{5}$ to a percent.

$$\begin{array}{r} .2 = 20\% \\ 5\overline{)1.0} \\ -1\,0 \\ \hline 0 \end{array}$$

Change each fraction to a percent. Show your work.

1. $\frac{1}{10} =$ **2.** $\frac{5}{100} =$ **3.** $\frac{7}{8} =$

4. $\frac{7}{20} =$ **5.** $\frac{3}{20} =$ **6.** $\frac{3}{4} =$

7. $\frac{11}{20} =$ **8.** $\frac{9}{10} =$ **9.** $\frac{4}{5} =$

CRITICAL THINKING

Fill in the missing numbers.

Fraction or Mixed Number	Decimal	Percent
$\frac{1}{5}$	?	?
?	1.25	?
?	?	75%

▶ 11.9 Finding the Percent   Exercise 107

> To find the percent, divide the part by the whole.
> Remember, the whole in a percent problem follows the word *of*.
>
> What percent of 50 is 17.50? $.35 = 35\%$
>   ↑   ↑ $50\overline{)17.50}$
>   Whole   Part $-15\,0$
> $2\,50$
> $-2\,50$
> 0

Find the percent in each problem.

1. 6 is what percent of 25?   **2.** 3 is what percent of 4?

3. 7 is what percent of 8?   **4.** 3 is what percent of 5?

5. What percent of 5 is 13?   **6.** What percent of 10 is 7?

7. What percent of 80 is 15?   **8.** What percent of 75 is 225?

CRITICAL THINKING

A pair of shoes costs $48. The discount on the shoes is $24.
What percent of the regular price is the discount?

▶ 11.10 Finding the Percent Increase/Decrease

To find a percent increase/decrease, first you need to find the difference. Then divide by the original amount.

Last month, Samantha's sales were $4,000. This month, her sales were $5,000. What is the percent increase?

Find the difference. $5,000 − $4,000 = $1,000

Divide the difference by last month's sales.

$\dfrac{\$1,000}{\$4,000}$ Difference
Original

$$\begin{array}{r} .25 = 25\% \\ 4,000\overline{)1,000.00} \\ -\ 800\ 0 \\ \hline 200\ 00 \\ -\ 200\ 00 \\ \hline 0 \end{array}$$

Solve to find the percent increase or decrease.

1. Lisa's sales are $1,600 this month. Last month, her sales were $2,000. What is the percent decrease?

2. A used bike sells for $60. Originally, it was $150. What is the percent decrease?

3. After 3 years of use, a $15,000 car decreases in value by $6,000. What is the percent decrease?

4. Bill's commission was $1,000 last month. This month, his commission is $1,250. What is the percent increase?

CRITICAL THINKING

How can you tell if the percent is a percent increase or a percent decrease?

11.11 Finding the Whole   Exercise 109

To find the whole in a percent problem, divide the part by the percent.

15 is 40% of what number?   40% = .40

↑   ↑
Part   Percent

$$
\begin{array}{r}
37.5 \\
.40\,\overline{)15.00.0} \\
-12\,0 \\
\hline
3\,00 \\
-2\,80 \\
\hline
200 \\
-200 \\
\hline
0
\end{array}
$$

Solve to find the whole in each problem.

1. 20% of what number is 5?   **2.** 15% of what number is 21?

3. 35% of what number is 91?   **4.** 50% of what number is 75?

5. 78 is 65% of what number?   **6.** 102 is 85% of what number?

7. 200% of what number is 30?   **8.** 150 is 75% of what number?

CRITICAL THINKING

At A&B Emporium, 50% of the employees take a bus to get to work. Every day 100 employees take the bus. How many employees work at Glow Emporium? Show your work.

▶ 11.12 Finding the Original Price   Exercise 110

To find the original price, first you need to find the percent of the original price.

A coat is on sale for $90. This is 25% off the original price. What was the original price?

25% *off* means 75% *of* the original price. $100\% - 25\% = 75\%$

Divide the sale price by the percent you found.

$$\begin{array}{r} 120 \rightarrow \$120 \\ .75\overline{)90.00} \\ -\,75 \\ \hline 150 \\ -\,150 \\ \hline 00 \end{array}$$

Find the original price in each problem.

1. A computer is 25% off the original price. The sale price is $900. What was the original price of the computer?

2. Mr. Cook bought parts for his car at 30% off the original price. He paid $35 for the parts. What was the original price?

3. A shirt was on sale for $17. This is 15% off the original price. What was the original price?

4. A computer game is on sale for $80. This is 20% off the original price. What was the original price of the game?

CRITICAL THINKING

An item is on sale for $100. Find each original price.

1. What is the original price if this is 20% off the original price?

2. What is the original price if this is 80% off the original price?

▶ 11.13 Problem Solving: Exercise 111
Finding the Part, Percent, or Whole

To solve a percent problem, decide what is given. Then find the missing piece.

Sue answered 75% of the quiz questions correctly. She answered 15 questions correctly. How many questions were on the quiz?

READ   *75% of the questions is 15.*

PLAN   Find the whole.

DO   Whole = Part ÷ Percent

$$.75\overline{)15.00} \quad \text{20 questions}$$
$$-\ 15\ 0$$
$$\overline{00}$$

Solve. Show your work.

1. Matt tried to make 15 baskets in a game. He made 40% of the baskets he tried. How many baskets did he make?

2. Jamille tried to make 15 baskets and made 12. What percent of her attempts were successful?

3. On Friday, 75 teachers showed up at West High. This is 75% of the entire staff. How many teachers work at Wright?

4. At a factory, 6% of the computer chips that are made will not work. One day, 650 chips were made. How many of the computer chips will not work?

5. On Monday, 108 cases of paper were loaded onto a truck. This is 45% of the shipment. How many cases of paper were in the shipment?

▶ 12.1 What Is a Ratio?   Exercise 112

A ratio compares two quantities. The order of numbers in a ratio is important.

Write the ratio of squares to total shapes.

There are 4 squares and 6 shapes. $\frac{4}{6}$ or   4:6   or   4 to 6

Ratios are written in lowest terms. $\frac{2}{3}$ or   2:3   or   2 to 3

Write each ratio with a ratio sign and as a fraction in lowest terms. Use the picture to find the ratios in Questions 1 and 2.

1. total shapes to circles

2. triangles to total shapes

3. vowels to number of letters in the word MONUMENT

4. total number of letters to vowels in the word ABSENT

5. number of I's to total number of letters in the word MISSISSIPPI

6. total number of letters to number of S's in the word MISSISSIPPI

CRITICAL THINKING

A math teacher lost her quiz about ratios. All she found were the shapes on the right and the ratios below. Which shapes could each ratio compare?

1. 2:3   2. 3:2   3. $\frac{2}{5}$ 4. $\frac{5}{3}$

▶ 12.2 What Is a Proportion?   Exercise 113

Two ratios form a proportion when the cross products are equal.

Write a ratio of the shaded parts to all parts for each circle. Do the ratios form a proportion?

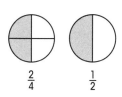

$\frac{2}{4}$ ⤬ $\frac{1}{2}$

$$2 \times 2 = 4 \qquad 4 \times 1 = 4$$
$$4 \;=\; 4 \checkmark \text{ Yes}$$

Decide if each pair of ratios forms a proportion. Write *Yes* or *No*.

1. $\frac{3}{4}$ $\frac{4}{6}$ _____

2. $\frac{3}{3}$ $\frac{5}{5}$ _____

3. $\frac{2}{3}$ $\frac{8}{12}$ _____

4. $\frac{4}{5}$ $\frac{8}{10}$ _____

5. $\frac{6}{8}$ $\frac{3}{4}$ _____

6. $\frac{2}{5}$ $\frac{3}{6}$ _____

7. $\frac{9}{12}$ $\frac{2}{3}$ _____

8. $\frac{1}{4}$ $\frac{3}{12}$ _____

9. $\frac{7}{10}$ $\frac{3}{4}$ _____

10. $\frac{16}{48}$ $\frac{1}{4}$ _____

11. $\frac{1}{5}$ $\frac{6}{30}$ _____

12. $\frac{9}{11}$ $\frac{8}{10}$ _____

13. $\frac{6}{9}$ $\frac{10}{15}$ _____

14. $\frac{1}{2}$ $\frac{12}{24}$ _____

15. $\frac{3}{4}$ $\frac{4}{3}$ _____

CRITICAL THINKING

Match each ratio in Column A with the ratio in Column B that will make a proportion.

Column A

1. $\frac{3}{4}$

2. $\frac{20}{25}$

3. $\frac{5}{6}$

Column B

a. $\frac{4}{5}$

b. $\frac{10}{12}$

c. $\frac{12}{16}$

12.3 Solving Proportions   Exercise 114

Use the cross product to find the missing number in a proportion.

Find the missing number in the proportion. $\frac{4}{5} = \frac{12}{?}$

Find a cross product. $5 \times 12 = 60$
Divide by the other number. $60 \div 4 = 15$
Check. $5 \times 12 = 4 \times 15$

                                 $60 = 60$ ✓

The missing number in the proportion is 15.

Find the missing number in each proportion. Check your work.

1. $\frac{3}{4} = \frac{?}{20}$ 2. $\frac{?}{5} = \frac{9}{15}$ 3. $\frac{9}{?} = \frac{11}{11}$

4. $\frac{8}{12} = \frac{?}{3}$ 5. $\frac{5}{7} = \frac{?}{35}$ 6. $\frac{1}{6} = \frac{4}{?}$

7. $\frac{?}{40} = \frac{5}{8}$ 8. $\frac{2}{?} = \frac{4}{6}$ 9. $\frac{2}{3} = \frac{20}{?}$

10. $\frac{2}{5} = \frac{?}{50}$ 11. $\frac{75}{100} = \frac{?}{4}$ 12. $\frac{12}{12} = \frac{17}{?}$

13. $\frac{4}{5} = \frac{?}{100}$ 14. $\frac{?}{3} = \frac{5}{15}$ 15. $\frac{3}{?} = \frac{1}{6}$

CRITICAL THINKING

Complete each proportion using two of the numbers from the choices below.

3   4   5   6   9   8

1. $\frac{?}{6} = \frac{6}{?}$ 2. $\frac{?}{10} = \frac{3}{?}$ 3. $\frac{1}{?} = \frac{?}{24}$

▶ 12.4 Multiple Unit Pricing   Exercise 115

> You can use a proportion to find prices or how many items you can buy.
>
> Tomatoes cost $3 for 2 pounds. How many pounds can you buy for $4.50?
>
> Set up a proportion and solve. $\dfrac{\$3}{2 \text{ pound}} = \dfrac{\$4.50}{? \text{ pounds}}$
>
> $4.50 \times 2 = 9$
> $9 \div 3 = 3$ pounds
>
> You can buy 3 pounds of tomatoes for $4.50.

Solve each problem using a proportion.

1. If 3 CDs sell for $25, how much do 15 CDs cost?

2. Fruit costs $2 dollars per pound. How many pounds can you buy for $1.50?

3. Two boxes of spaghetti cost $.70. How much do five boxes of spaghetti cost?

4. Potting soil costs $4.00 for 5 pounds. How much potting soil can you buy for $10?

5. A pound of apples costs $.85. How many pounds can you buy for $6.00?

CRITICAL THINKING

What is wrong with the sale price in this picture?

> **SALE!!**
> Batteries
> *Now 2 for $3.*
> Before sale
> 4 for $5.

Name _____ Date _____

Use proportions to find actual sizes in scale drawings.

Find the actual length of the kitchen.

$$\frac{1 \text{ in.}}{20 \text{ ft}} \nearrow \frac{1\frac{1}{2} \text{ in.}}{? \text{ ft}}$$

$$20 \times 1\frac{1}{2} = 30$$

$$30 \div 1 = 30 \text{ feet}$$

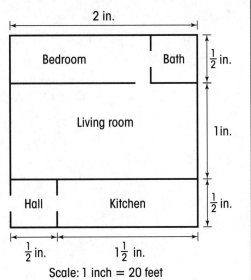

Scale: 1 inch = 20 feet

Use the scale drawing at the top of the page to find the actual length or width.

1. the length of the living room

2. the length of the hall

3. the width of the kitchen

4. the width of the living room

5. the length of the bedroom

6. the width of the bedroom

CRITICAL THINKING

This is a drawing of a building that is 60 feet wide and 20 feet high. What scale was used to create the picture?

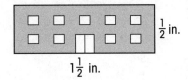

1 inch = _____

▶ 12.6 Problem Solving: Using Proportions   Exercise 117

Use proportions to solve word problems.

A part of a quilt has 5 white squares and 4 red squares. There are 36 red squares in the whole quilt. How many white squares are there in the whole quilt?

PLAN   Write a proportion. $\dfrac{5 \text{ white}}{4 \text{ red}} = \dfrac{? \text{ white}}{36 \text{ red}}$

DO   Solve the proportion. $5 \times 36 = 180$
                                        $180 \div 4 = 45$ white squares

There are 45 white squares in the whole quilt.

READ the problem. Make a PLAN. DO the plan to solve the problem.

1. A 5-pound pumpkin costs $3.50. How much does a
   3-pound pumpkin cost?

2. A photo is 4 inches by 6 inches. The photo is enlarged
   so the longer side is now 9 inches. How long is the shorter
   side now?

3. A copier can make 50 copies in 2 minutes. How long does it
   take to make 75 copies?

4. It takes 3 sprinklers to cover 200 square feet of grass. How
   many sprinklers does it take to cover 1,000 square feet?

5. A marathon runner can run 5 miles in 25 minutes. How
   many miles can he run in 60 minutes if he continues
   running at the same pace?

6. Joe reads about 250 pages per week. How long does it take
   him to read a 750-page book?

Name_____   Date_____

A **pictograph** uses pictures to represent quantities. To make a pictograph, you need to assign a number to a picture. This is the key. Then draw as many pictures as you need.

Licensed Drivers by Age (rounded numbers)	
Age	Drivers
Under 19	10,000,000
20–39	75,000,000
40–59	60,000,000
60–79	30,000,000
Over 80	5,000,000

Licensed Drivers by Age

Under 19	☨
20–39	☨ ☨ ☨ ☨ ☨ ☨ ⸝
40–59	☨ ☨ ☨ ☨ ☨
60–79	☨ ☨ ☨
Over 80	⸝

Key: ☨ = 10,000,000 drivers

Make a pictograph of the information in each table.

1. Round to the nearest hundred.

Number of Public Libraries 1993	
Kansas	320
Missouri	148
Nebraska	269
Oklahoma	110

2. Round the the nearest million.

World Motor Vehicle Production	
Canada	2,570,000
Europe	17,770,000
Japan	10,980,000
United States	12,120,000
Other	10,020,000

CRITICAL THINKING

Use the pictograph of licensed drivers to answer each question.

1. Which age group has the greatest number of licensed drivers? How do you know?

2. How many drivers does half a figure represent?

Name_____ Date_____

▶ 13.2 Single Bar Graphs   Exercise 119

A **bar graph** uses bars to represent quantities.

Weekly Hours Worked	
Name	Hours
Brian	35
Judy	50
Tony	40

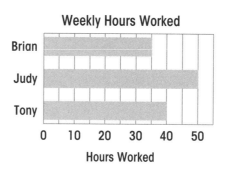

Make a horizontal bar graph.

Ice Cream Sold	
Month	Gallons
April	125
May	150
June	275
July	300

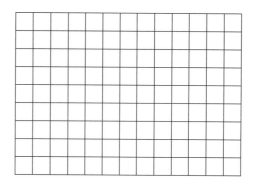

CRITICAL THINKING

Make a vertical bar graph.

Sunny Days in Miami	
Season	Days
Winter	40
Spring	55
Summer	65
Fall	45

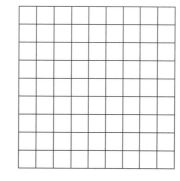

Name _____ Date _____

Use a **double bar** graph to compare two sets of data for the same item.

Weekly Hours Worked		
Name	Week 1	Week 2
Brian	35	40
Judy	50	45
Tony	40	35

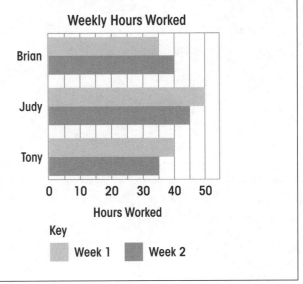

Make a horizontal double bar graph.

Football Games Won		
Team	1997	1998
Wildcats	9	10
Lumberjacks	7	8
Sun Devils	11	8

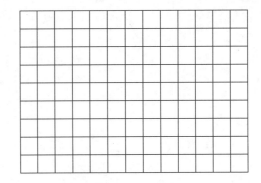

CRITICAL THINKING

Make a vertical double bar graph.

Tickets Sold		
Show	7:00	9:00
A	30	40
B	45	25
C	40	45

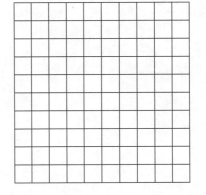

Name _____ Date _____

▶ 13.4 Single Line Graphs   Exercise 121

Line graphs are used to show change over a period of time.

XYZ Corporation (rounded numbers)	
Year	Employees
1960	75,000
1970	175,000
1980	175,000
1990	200,000
2000	225,000

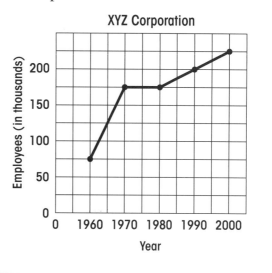

Make a line graph.

Rainfall	
Month	Rainfall (inches)
January	4.0
February	4.5
March	3.5
April	2.0
May	2.5

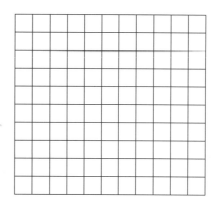

CRITICAL THINKING

Use the graph of the XYZ Corporation to answer each question.

1. Between which two years does the graph show the greatest increase in the number of employees? How do you know?

2. Between which two years did the number of employees stay about the same? How do you know?

3. About how many employees worked at the XYZ corporation in 1965?

▶ 13.5 Double Line Graphs

Use a **double line graph** to compare two sets of data over time.

Corporation Employees (rounded numbers)		
Year	XYZ	ABC
1960	75,000	125,000
1970	175,000	175,000
1980	175,000	150,000
1990	200,000	175,000
2000	225,000	200,000

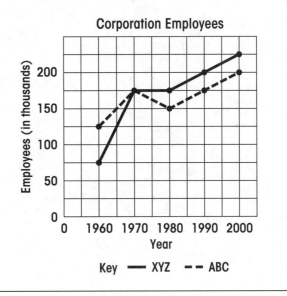

Make a double line graph.

Sales		
Month	Tapes	CDs
January	200	300
February	250	250
March	450	400
April	400	350
May	300	200
June	350	400

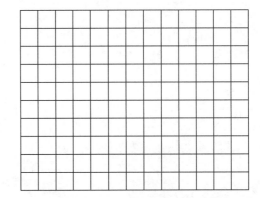

CRITICAL THINKING

Use the graph of the two corporations above to answer each question.

1. When did both corporations have about the same number of employees?

2. Between which two years did the number of employees decrease for the ABC corporation?

Name _____ Date _____

▶ **13.6 Problem Solving: Choosing a Scale**   **Exercise 123**

Changing the scale of a graph can change its message.

The Book Store wants to show that its sales are increasing. Which graph should they use and why?

PLAN   Compare the graphs.
Which line looks like it is increasing by a greater amount?

DO   Look at Graph A. The increase looks greater because the scale is smaller.

The Book Store should use Graph A.

In which graph below does the minimum wage appear to be changing more slowly? Why?

▶ 13.7 Circle Graphs   Exercise 124

Use **circle graphs** to show how the total amount (100%) is divided.

There are 500 students in Roosevelt school.
How many students ride a bicycle to school?

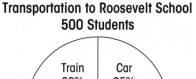

**Transportation to Roosevelt School
500 Students**

Look at the graph.
Of the 500 students,
10% ride a bicycle to school.
Multiply.

$.10 \times 500 = 50$

50 students ride a bicycle to school.

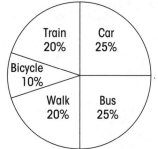

Use the above graph to answer each question.

1. What percent of the students walk to school?

2. How many students walk to school?

3. How many students take a bus to school?

4. How many more students take a car to school than a train?

CRITICAL THINKING

Use the graph on the right to answer each question.

1. What percent of the students in Lincoln
   High are in the 12th grade?

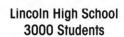

**Lincoln High School
3000 Students**

2. Which grade has the greatest number
   of students?

3. How many more students are in the 11th
   grade than in the 9th grade?

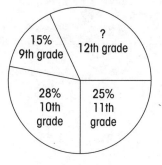

13.8 Mean (Average)   Exercise 125

> The **mean** is an average. The average describes the typical number in a set.
>
> $$\text{Mean} = \frac{\text{Sum of the numbers}}{\text{Number of numbers}}$$
>
> Alex's test grades in English are 73, 88, 75, and 92. What is his mean test grade?
>
> $$\text{Mean} = \frac{73 + 88 + 75 + 92}{4} = \frac{328}{4} = 82$$
>
> Alex's mean test grade in English is 82%.

Find the mean of each set of numbers.

1. 7, 7, 8, 10, 13   **2.** 16, 18, 25, 25, 30

3. 3.5, 6.5, 7, 8, 10.5   **4.** 120, 125, 129, 130

5. 58, 784, 1003   **6.** 35, 40, 25, 56, 47

7. 58, 72, 115, 128, 147   **8.** 6.5, 7.2, 7.6, 11.6, 12.1

CRITICAL THINKING

Joe compares the prices of a pair of jeans. He goes to four different stores.

1. What is the mean (average) price?

2. How much is the least expensive pair of jeans?

Store	Price
A	$26.95
B	$24.95
C	$28.95
D	$30.00

3. A fifth store is having a going-out-of-business sale. The jeans there are $15.00. Joe includes this price in his chart. Will this new price increase or decrease the mean?

Name_____   Date_____

▶ 13.9 Median and Mode   Exercise 126

The **median** is the middle number when a set of numbers is in order from least to greatest. If there is an even number of numbers, the median is the average of the two middle numbers.

Find the median.   15 18 17 19 10 12

    Place the numbers in order.   10 12 15 17 18 19

    Find the average of the two
        middle numbers: $\dfrac{15 + 17}{2} = \dfrac{32}{2} = 16$

The median is 16.

The **mode** is the number that occurs most often.

Find the mode.   **5** 8 6 **5** 4 **5**

The mode is 5.

Find the median of each set of numbers.

1. 85, 48, 75, 36, 55

2. 147, 84, 211, 254, 159, 198

3. 25, 56, 84, 54

4. 357, 254, 541, 472, 105

5. 24, 28, 31, 25, 35, 39, 27

6. 2.5, 3.8, 4.8, 2.9, 3.1

Find the mode of each set of numbers.

7. 12, 54, 34, 18, 42, 34

8. 24, 65, 23, 58, 58, 23, 54

9. 508, 457, 685, 305

10. 5.5, 5.8, 5.4, 5.7, 5.8, 5.1

CRITICAL THINKING

Write a set of numbers where the mean, median, and mode are the same number.

126   Chapter 13 • Graphs and Statistics

Copyright © by Globe Fearon, Inc. All rights reserved.

▶ 13.10 Histograms   Exercise 127

A **histogram** is a graph that shows how many items occur between two numbers.

The Springfield Library has books arranged by grade level.

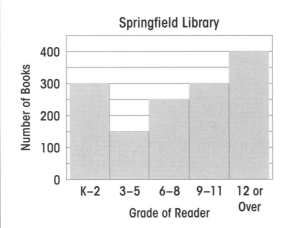

Springfield Library

How many books are there for grades 6–11?

Find the number of books for grades 6–8.   250
Find the number of books for grades 9–11.   300
Add to find the books for grades 6–11.   250 + 300 = 550

There are 550 books for grades 6–11.

Use the histogram above to answer each question.

1. How many books are there for grades 3–5?

2. Which grade levels have the greatest number of books?

3. Which grade levels have the fewest number of books?

4. How many books are there for students in grades 6 and above?

5. How many books are in the Springfield Library?

CRITICAL THINKING

What percent of all of the books in the histogram are for grades 9 and above?

▶ 13.11 Probability   Exercise 128

Probability is the chance that something will happen.

$$\text{Probability} = \frac{\text{Number of favorable outcomes}}{\text{Total number of outcomes}}$$

A bag has 2 blue, 3 red, 1 yellow, and 4 green marbles.
What is the probability of picking a green marble?

| Number of favorable outcomes | 4 green marbles |
| Total number of outcomes | 10 marbles altogether |

Write the probability as a fraction. $\frac{4}{10} = \frac{2}{5}$

Find the probability of each outcome. Use the spinner pictured below.

1. the probability of picking 1

2. the probability of picking 6

3. the probability of picking a multiple of 4

4. the probability of picking an odd number

5. the probability of picking a prime number

The letters of the word PRECIPITATION are put in a box. Find the probability

6. of picking an R.   **7.** of picking an A.   **8.** of picking a P.

9. of picking a T.   **10.** of picking an I.   **11.** of picking a vowel.

CRITICAL THINKING

You are taking a multiple-choice test. Each item has 4 choices.
What is the probability that you will guess the correct choice?

14.1 Length

> To change a larger unit to a smaller unit, multiply.
>
> Change 10 yards to inches.
> Multiply yards by 36.
> $36 \times 10 = 360$ inches
>
> To change a smaller unit to a larger unit, divide.
>
> Change 48 inches to feet.
> Divide inches by 12.
> $48 \div 12 = 4$ feet

Useful Facts
1 foot = 12 inches
1 yard = 36 inches
1 yard = 3 feet
1 mile = 5,280 feet
1 mile = 1,760 yards

Change each measurement. First decide whether to multiply or divide.

1. 3 miles = _____ yards
2. 7 feet = _____ inches
3. 5 yards = _____ inches

4. $4\frac{1}{2}$ yards = _____ feet
5. 2 miles = _____ feet
6. $4\frac{1}{2}$ feet = _____ inches

7. 12 feet = _____ yards
8. 60 inches = _____ feet
9. 96 inches = _____ yards

10. 18 inches = _____ feet
11. 33 feet = _____ yards
12. 7,040 yards = _____ miles

13. 100 inches = _____ feet
14. 5 miles = _____ yards
15. $7\frac{1}{2}$ yards = _____ feet

16. 80 feet = _____ yards
17. 17 yards = _____ inches
18. $2\frac{1}{4}$ feet = _____ yards

CRITICAL THINKING

Write the missing units.

1. 45 feet = 15 _____
2. 6 feet = 72 _____
3. 10,560 feet = 2 _____

14.2 Weight

To change a larger unit to a smaller unit, multiply.

Change $1\frac{1}{4}$ tons to pounds.
Multiply tons by 2,000.
$1\frac{1}{4} \times 2,000 = 2,500$ pounds

Useful Facts	
1 pound	= 16 ounces
1 ton	= 2,000 pounds

To change a smaller unit to a larger unit, divide.

Change 32 ounces to pounds.
Divide ounces by 16.
$32 \div 16 = 2$ pounds

Change each measurement. First, decide whether to multiply or divide.

1. 5 tons = ___ pounds

2. 8 pounds = ___ ounces

3. 10 tons = ___ pounds

4. $4\frac{1}{4}$ pounds = ___ ounces

5. $5\frac{1}{2}$ tons = ___ pounds

6. 10 pounds = ___ ounces

7. 80 ounces = ___ pounds

8. 4,000 pounds = ___ tons

9. 40 ounces = ___ pounds

10. 1,500 pounds = ___ tons

CRITICAL THINKING

Choose the best answer.

A box of cereal weighs about 24 ounces. This is the same as
  a. .072 ton
  b. 384 pounds
  c. $1\frac{1}{2}$ pounds

▶ 14.3 Capacity (Liquid Measure)   Exercise 131

To change a larger unit to a smaller unit, multiply.

Change 5 quarts to pints.
Multiply quarts by 2.
$5 \times 2 = 10$ pints

To change a smaller unit to a larger unit, divide.

Change 40 fluid ounces to quarts.
Divide fluid ounces by 32.
$40 \div 32 = 1\frac{1}{4}$ quarts

Useful Facts	
1 pint	= 16 fluid ounces
1 quart	= 32 fluid ounces
1 quart	= 2 pints
1 gallon	= 4 quarts

Change each measurement. First, decide whether to multiply or divide.

1. 4.5 gallons = _____ quarts

2. 7 pints = _____ fluid ounces

3. 3 quarts = _____ fluid ounces

4. $8\frac{1}{2}$ quarts = _____ pints

5. 32 fluid ounces = _____ pints

6. 20 quarts = _____ gallons

7. 9 pints = _____ quarts

8. 48 fluid ounces = _____ quarts

9. 12 quarts = _____ pints

10. 68 fluid ounces = _____ quarts

11. 12 gallons = _____ quarts

12. 15 pints = _____ quarts

CRITICAL THINKING

Choose a word, *gallon* or *pint*, to fill in each blank.

1. A large container of milk holds 1 _____.

2. A small pot contains about 1 _____ of soup.

▶ 14.4 Time

To change a larger unit to a smaller unit, multiply.

Change 3 years to months.
Multiply years by 12.
$3 \times 12 = 36$ months

To change a smaller unit to a larger unit, divide.

Change 420 minutes to hours.
Divide minutes by 60.
$420 \div 60 = 7$ hours

Useful Facts	
60 seconds	= 1 minute
60 minutes	= 1 hour
24 hours	= 1 day
7 days	= 1 week
52 weeks	= 1 year
12 months	= 1 year

Change each measurement. First, decide whether to multiply or divide.

1. 3 years = _____ weeks

2. 12 hours = _____ minutes

3. $1\frac{1}{2}$ days = _____ hours

4. $1\frac{1}{4}$ years = _____ months

5. 130 weeks = _____ years

6. 48 months = _____ years

7. 90 minutes = _____ hours

8. 36 hours = _____ days

9. 26 weeks = _____ years

10. 90 minutes = _____ seconds

11. $3\frac{1}{2}$ years = _____ months

12. 15 minutes = _____ hour

CRITICAL THINKING

How many hours are in a week? Explain.

▶ 14.5 Problem Solving: Exercise 133
Working with Units of Measure

Sometimes you need to change from one unit of measure to another unit.

Laura made 3 dozen cookies. A dozen cookies weighs 10 ounces. A box can hold 1 pound of cookies. Remember, 1 pound = 16 ounces.
Will 2 boxes be enough to hold 3 dozen cookies?

PLAN   Find how many ounces in 3 dozen cookies.
          Find how many ounces 2 boxes can hold. Compare.

DO   Multiply. 3×10 ounces = 30 ounces
            Change 2 pounds to ounces. 2×16 ounces = 32 ounces
            Compare.   30 ounces < 32 ounces

The 2 boxes will be enough to hold 3 dozen cookies.

READ the problem. Make a PLAN. DO the plan to solve the problem.

1. Phuong ran three times this week. She ran 2 miles, 880 yards, and $2\frac{1}{2}$ miles. Remember, 1 mile = 1,760 yards. How many miles did she run altogether?

2. Each day, Mr. Re teaches 4 math classes. Each class is 45 minutes long. He also teachers a computer class for 1 hour. Remember, 1 hour = 60 minutes. How many hours does he teach each day?

3. Renelle is knitting a scarf. It is supposed to be 4 feet long. So far, she has knitted 30 inches. Remember, 1 foot = 12 inches. How many more inches does she have to knit?

4. Ken is going to mix paint in a large container. The container holds 3 gallons. There are 5 quarts of blue paint, 8 quarts of yellow, and 2 quarts of white. Remember, 1 gallon = 4 quarts. Will the container hold all of the paint?

▶ 14.6 Elapsed Time

To find elapsed time, you must subtract. Rename if necessary.

Find elapsed time from 7:15 A.M. to 8:10 A.M.	Find elapsed time from 9:00 P.M. to 3:15 A.M.

$$\begin{array}{r} 7 \quad 70 \\ \cancel{8}\,\text{hr} \; \cancel{10}\,\text{min} \\ -\,7\,\text{hr}\;\;15\,\text{min} \\ \hline 0\,\text{hr}\;\;55\,\text{min} \end{array}$$

$$\begin{array}{l} 15 \quad \longleftarrow \text{Add 12 hours.} \\ \cancel{3}\text{:}15\;\text{A.M.} \\ -9\text{:}00\;\text{P.M.} \\ \hline 6\text{:}15 \longrightarrow 6\,\text{hr}\;15\,\text{min} \end{array}$$

Find the elapsed time.

1. 8:15 A.M. to 11:30 A.M.   2. 5:20 P.M. to 11 P.M.   3. 7:55 A.M. to 12 noon

4. 6:30 P.M. to 7:20 P.M.   5. 1:00 A.M. to 1:00 P.M.   6. 12:30 P.M. to 4:45 P.M.

7. The bus picks up students at 7:30 A.M. and arrives at school at 8:15 A.M. How long is the trip to school?

8. The third shift starts at 10 P.M. and ends at 5:15 A.M. How long is the shift?

CRITICAL THINKING

Find each end time.

1. It is 8:20 A.M. What time will it be after 1 hour and 20 minutes has elapsed?

2. It is 9:20 A.M. What time will it be after 3 hours and 40 minutes has elapsed?

▶ 14.7 Temperature   Exercise 135

> Add if the temperature rises. Subtract if the temperature drops or falls.
>
> At noon the temperature was 85°. Then it fell 3°. What was the new temperature?
>
> The word *fell* tells you to subtract.   85° − 3° = 82°

Add or subtract to find the new temperature. To decide, look for the words *rise* and *fall*.

1. At 10 P.M. the temperature outside was 65°. Overnight, the temperature fell 15°. What was the temperature in the morning?

2. The temperature in the morning was 65°. Then the temperature rose 9°. What was the new temperature?

3. The temperature in the apartment was 60°. Then the air conditioner was turned off. The temperature rose 12° in 7 hours. What was the new temperature?

4. The temperature of the ocean was 70° in June. In October, the temperature was 15° lower. What was the temperature in October?

CRITICAL THINKING

Fill in each missing word with *rose* or *fell*.

1. At 7 A.M. the temperature was 28°. By noon, the temperature was 32°.

   The temperature _____ 4°.

2. The temperature of the oven was 375°. Luis took the bread out of the oven. The oven cooled to 275°.

   The oven temperature _____ 100°.

Name _____   Date _____

▶ **15.1 What Is the Metric System?**   **Exercise 136**

The metric system has three basic units. A meter is used to measure length. A gram is used to measure weight. A liter is used to measure capacity. Prefixes in front of a base tell you how many units there are.

Prefix	Value	Prefix	Value
kilo-	1,000	deci-	.1
hecto-	100	centi-	.01
deka-	10	milli-	.001

Answer each question. Use the chart above to help you.

1. How many meters in a kilometer?   **2.** How many grams in a hectogram?

3. How many liters in a dekaliter?   **4.** How much of a gram is a decigram?

5. How much of a liter is a milliliter?   **6.** How much of a meter is a centimeter?

7. How many liters in a kiloliter?   **8.** How many grams in a dekagram?

CRITICAL THINKING

1. The distance around a baseball diamond is about .1 kilometer. About how many meters is this?

2. The amount of milk contained in a glass is 200 milliliters. About how many liters is this?

3. A new pink eraser has a mass of about 2 grams. About how many milligrams is this?

136   Chapter 15 • Metric Measurement

▶ 15.2 Length

In the metric system, the meter is used to measure length.

Largest → → → → → Smallest
km hm dam m dm cm mm

To change a larger unit to a smaller unit, multiply.

Change 5.6 kilometers to meters.
Multiply kilometers by 1,000.
$5.6 \times 1,000 = 5,600$ meters

To change a smaller unit to a larger unit, divide.

Change 89 meters to kilometers.
Divide meters by 1,000.
$89 \div 1,000 = .089$ kilometer

Useful Facts	
1 kilometer	= 1,000 meters
1 hectometer	= 100 meters
1 dekameter	= 10 meters
1 meter	= 1 meter
10 decimeters	= 1 meter
100 centimeters	= 1 meter
1,000 millimeters	= 1 meter

Change each measurement. First, decide whether to multiply or divide.

1. 9 kilometers = _____ meters

2. 3 centimeters = _____ millimeters

3. 12 meters = _____ centimeters

4. 100 meters = _____ millimeters

5. 1,054 meters = _____ kilometers

6. 6,000 millimeters = _____ meters

7. 50 centimeters = _____ meter

8. 40 decimeters = _____ dekameter

9. 9.2 centimeters = _____ millimeters

10. 1.2 meters = _____ millimeters

11. 35 meters = _____ hectometer

12. 15 millimeters = _____ centimeter

CRITICAL THINKING

1. The circumference of a baseball is 238 millimeters. How many centimeters is that?

2. A relay race is 1.5 kilometers long. How many meters is that?

15.3 Mass

In the metric system, the gram is used to measure mass.

Largest → → → → → Smallest
kg   hg   dag   **g**   dg   cg   mg

To change a larger unit to a smaller unit, multiply.

Change 80 grams to centigrams.
Multiply grams by 100.
$80 \times 100 = 8,000$ centigrams

To change a smaller unit to a larger unit, divide.

Change 4 grams to dekagrams.
Divide grams by 10.
$4 \div 10 = .4$ dekagram

Useful Facts	
1 kilogram	= 1,000 grams
1 hectogram	= 100 grams
1 dekagram	= 10 grams
1 gram	= 1 gram
10 decigrams	= 1 gram
100 centigrams	= 1 gram
1,000 milligrams	= 1 gram

Change each measurement. First, decide whether to multiply or divide.

1. 3 kilograms = _____ grams

2. 10 grams = _____ milligrams

3. 48 grams = _____ centigrams

4. 25 hectograms = _____ grams

5. 50 grams = _____ kilogram

5. 800 milligrams = _____ gram

7. 485 grams = _____ dekagrams

8. 2,500 grams = _____ kilograms

9. 12 centigrams = _____ milligrams

10. 6 grams = _____ milligrams

11. 75 centigrams = _____ gram

12. 8,500 milligrams = _____ grams

CRITICAL THINKING

A large jar of sauce is about .5 kilograms.
This is about how many grams?

15.4 Capacity (Liquid Measure)   Exercise 139

In the metric system, the liter is used to measure liquid capacity.

Largest → → → → → Smallest
kL   hL   daL   L   dL   cL   mL

To change a larger unit to a smaller unit, multiply.

Change 23.4 kiloliters to liters.
Multiply kiloliters by 1,000.
$23.4 \times 1,000 = 23,400$

To change a smaller unit to a larger unit, divide.

Change 431 milliliters to centiliters.
Divide milliters by 10.
$431 \div 10 = 43.1$ centiliters

Useful Facts	
1 kiloliter	= 1,000 liters
1 hectoliter	= 100 liters
1 dekaliter	= 10 liters
1 liter	= 1 liter
10 deciliters	= 1 liter
100 centiliters	= 1 liter
1,000 milliliters	= 1 liter
10 milliliters	= 1 centiliter

Change each measurement. First, decide whether to multiply or divide.

1. 12 liters = _____ milliliters

2. 5.9 kiloliters = _____ liters

3. 4.6 liters = _____ centiliters

4. 9.8 liters = _____ deciliters

5. 760 milliliters = _____ liters

6. 600 centiliters = _____ liters

7. 4,800 liters = _____ kiloliters

8. 500 liters = _____ hectoliters

9. 3.4 kiloliters = _____ liters

10. 4 hectoliters = _____ liters

11. 60 liters = _____ dekaliters

12. 750 centiliters = _____ liters

CRITICAL THINKING

1. A fruit drink recipe calls for 1.5 liters of juice. How many milliliters is this?

2. The recipe calls for 250 millilters of fruit concentrate. How many liters is this?

Name _____ Date _____

▶ 15.5 Comparing Metric and Customary Measurements

Exercise 140

> You can use either customary or metric units to describe the length, weight, or capacity of an item.
>
> 2.5 centimeters is about 1 inch.   1 liter is about 1 quart.
>
> 1.6 kilometers is about 1 mile.   28 grams is about 1 ounce.

Complete each sentence.

1. 7.5 centimeters is about 3 ____.

2. 2 liters is about 2 ____.

3. 84 grams is about 3 ____.

4. 8 kilometers is about 5 ____.

5. 8 liters is about 8 ____ or 2 ____.

6. 15 centimeters is about 6 ____.

7. 16 kilometers is about 10 ____.

8. 168 grams is about 6 ____.

9. 14 grams is about ____.

10. 1.25 centimeters is about ____.

CRITICAL THINKING

Decide which units of measurement, both customary and metric, would make each statement true.

	Customary	Metric
1. The height of a mountain is about 3	_____	or about 4.8 _____.
2. The length of a book is about 25	_____	or about 10 _____.
3. A small container of milk is about 1	_____	or about 1 _____.
4. A box of spaghetti is about 450	_____	or about 16 _____.

Date _____

15.6 Problem Solving: Two-Part Problems

To solve two-part word problems, you may need to answer a hidden question.

Robin needs 5 meters of ribbon. The ribbon comes in rolls of 250 centimeters each. How many rolls will she have to buy?

PLAN   Find how many centimeters in 5 meters.
Remember 100 centimeters = 1 meter
Then divide to find how many rolls of ribbon to buy.

DO   Change 5 meters to centimeters. $5 \times 100 = 500$ centimers
Divide. $500 \div 250 = 2$ rolls

Robin will have to buy 2 rolls of ribbon.

READ the problem. Make a PLAN. DO the plan to solve the problem.

1. Armando's car can go 11.3 kilometers on 1 liter of fuel. The capacity of the car's fuel tank is 80 liters. How far can he drive if his tank is only $\frac{1}{2}$ full?

2. The mass of 1 nickel is about 5 grams. There are 40 nickels in a roll. Find the mass of 3 rolls of nickels?

3. Mr. Minor has to drive 1,710 kilometers. He drove 657 kilometers on the first day and 681 kilometers on the second day. How far does he still have to drive?

4. Al and Gail are wrapping 150 gifts for children who are in the hospital for the holidays. They use 30 centimeters of tape for each gift. Tape comes in rolls of 250 centimeters each. How many rolls of tape should they buy?

5. Amanda had 1 kilogram of flour. On Saturday, she used 300 grams of flour. On Sunday, she used 350 grams of the flour. How many grams of flour are left?

Name _____   Date _____

The table below shows some basic figures in geometry.

A •	point *A*
◄—•——•—► *A* *B*	line *AB*
•————————• *A* *B*	line segment *AB*
◄—•——————• *A* *B*	ray *BA*

Name each figure. Write *point*, *line*, *line segment*, or *ray*.

1.

2.

3. • *O*

4.

5.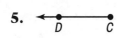

6.

Draw and label a picture for each name.

7. ray *AB*   8. point *X*   9. line segment *JK*

10. line *XO*   11. ray *GH*   12. line *YZ*

CRITICAL THINKING

1. What geometric figure would you use to show a city on a map?

2. What kind of figure would you use to draw the hand of a clock?

▶ 16.2 Measuring Angles   Exercise 143

> Use a protractor to measure an angle. Place the center of the protractor's straight edge on the vertex. One ray must pass through 0°.
>
>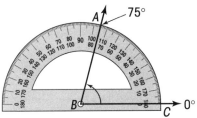
>
> Angle *ABC* measures 75°.

Use a protractor to measure each angle.

1.

2.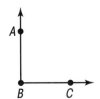

3.

4.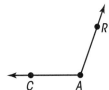

CRITICAL THINKING

Do not use your protractor. Label each angle 90°, 45°, or 155°.

1.

2.

3.

Name_____   Date_____

▶ 16.3 Drawing Angles   **Exercise 144**

You can use a protractor to draw angles.

Draw a 115° angle.
First draw a ray. Then locate 115° on the protractor.

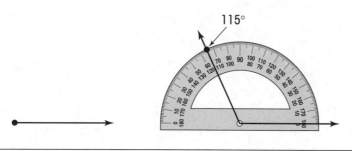

Use a protractor to draw an angle with each measure.

1. 65°   **2.** 125°   **3.** 15°

4. 45°   **5.** 80°   **6.** 140°

7. 25°   **8.** 105°   **9.** 75°

CRITICAL THINKING

Is the measure that is given for each angle too small or too large?

1. 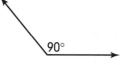   **2.**   **3.**

144   Chapter 16 • Geometry

▶ 16.4 Angles in a Triangle

Exercise 145

The sum of the angles in a triangle is always 180°.

Find the measure of the third angle in triangle *MNO*.

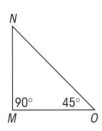

Find the sum of the known angles.	90°
	+ 45°
	135°

Subtract the sum from 180°.	180°
	− 135°
	45°

Find the measure of the third angle in each triangle.

1.

90° 40°

2.

25°   25°

3.

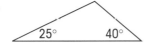

25°   40°

4.

← 54°

56°

5.

← 50°

75°

6.

42°   48°

7.

37°

23°

8.

← 60°

60°

CRITICAL THINKING

What is wrong with this picture?

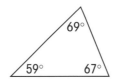

69°

59°   67°

Name_____ Date_____

Some polygons have special names.

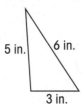

Scalene triangle
No sides are equal.

Isosceles triangle
At least two sides are equal.

Equilateral triangle
Three sides are equal.

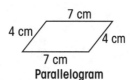

Parallelogram
A quadrilateral with the opposite
sides parallel and equal in length.

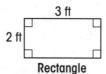

Rectangle
A parallelogram with all four
angles equal to 90°.

Square
A rectangle with
sides equal.

Name each polygon.

1.

_____

2.
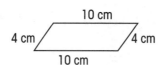

_____

3.

_____

4.
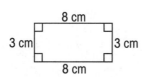

_____

5.

_____

6.

_____

CRITICAL THINKING

The first letter of the name of each polygon is given below. Complete each name.

1.

Q _____

2.

P _____

3.

O _____

Name _____ Date _____

▶ 16.6 Perimeter   Exercise 147

The **perimeter** is the total distance around a figure.

Find the perimeter of this rectangle.

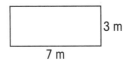

3 m

7 m

Add the lengths of all the sides.

7m + 7m + 3m + 3m = 20 meters

Find the perimeter of each figure.

1.

8 yd   8 yd

9 yd

2.

3 m

4 m

3.

12 in.

12 in.

4.

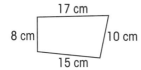

17 cm

8 cm   10 cm

15 cm

5.

2 in.   2 in.

2 in.   2 in.

2 in.   2 in.

6.

9 m   7 m

10 m   4 m

7 m

7.

.5 mm   .5 mm

.5 mm   .5 mm

.5 mm

8.

6 in.   6 in.

4 in.   4 in.

8 in.

9.

5 ft

10 ft

CRITICAL THINKING

Use the perimeter and picture to find the missing side of each figure.

1.

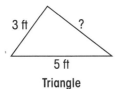

3 ft   ?

5 ft

Triangle

perimeter = 12 ft

2.

5 cm

?

5 cm

Rectangle

perimeter = 16 cm

3.

?

Square

perimeter = 20 in.

Name ______________________________ Date ______________________

16.7 Area of Squares and Rectangles — Exercise 148

To find the area of a rectangle, use this formula: Area = length × width.

Find the area of this rectangle.

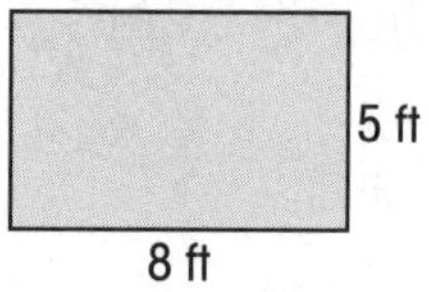
5 ft
8 ft

Area = length × width
Area = 8 ft × 5 ft
Area = 40 sq ft

Find the area of each figure.

1.
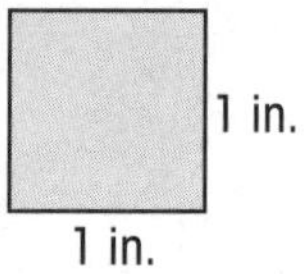
1 in.
1 in.

2.
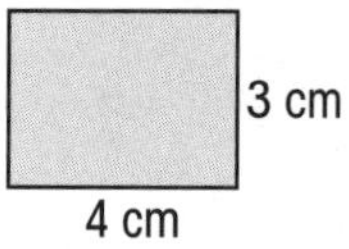
3 cm
4 cm

3.
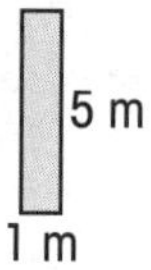
5 m
1 m

4.
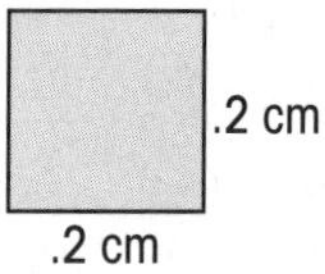
.2 cm
.2 cm

5.
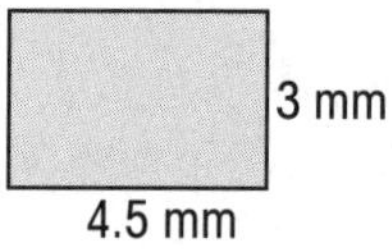
3 mm
4.5 mm

6.
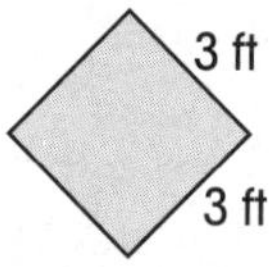
3 ft
3 ft

7.
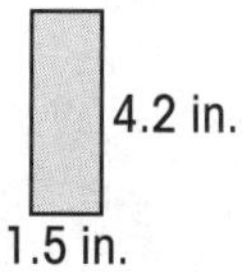
4.2 in.
1.5 in.

8.
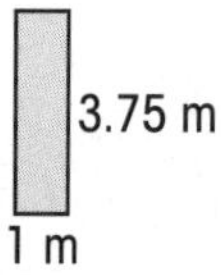
3.75 m
1 m

9.
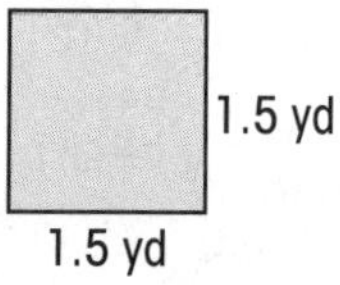
1.5 yd
1.5 yd

CRITICAL THINKING

Decide whether you would use perimeter or area to find the following.

1. the amount of fabric to cover a wall

2. the amount of chalk striping needed to outline a soccer field

▶ 16.8 Area of Parallelograms   Exercise 149

> To find the area of a parallelogram, use this formula: Area = base × height.
>
> Find the area of this parallelogram.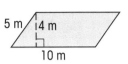
>
> Area = base × height
> Area = 10 m × 4 m
> Area = 40 sq m

Find the area of each figure.

1.

2.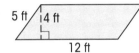

3.

4.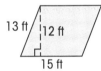

5.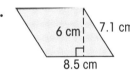

6.

CRITICAL THINKING

Match each figure with the correct perimeter and area.

1.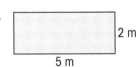

2.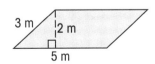

3.

a. $A = 10$ sq m
$P = 16$ m

b. $A = 16$ sq m
$P = 16$ m

c. $A = 10$ sq m
$P = 14$ m

▶ 16.9 Area of Triangles   Exercise 150

To find the area of a triangle, use this formula: Area $= \frac{1}{2} \times$ base $\times$ height

Find the area of this triangle.

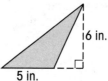

Area $= \frac{1}{2} \times$ base $\times$ height

Area $= \frac{1}{2} \times 5$ in. $\times 6$ in.

Area $= 15$ sq in.

Find the area of each triangle.

1.

2.

3.

4.

5.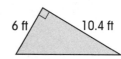

6.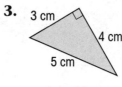

CRITICAL THINKING

The given area for each triangle is incorrect. Find the correct area. Explain how the mistake was made.

1.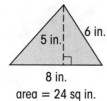

area = 24 sq in.

2.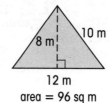

area = 96 sq m

3.

area = 10 sq cm

Name _____ Date _____

The **circumference** of a circle is the distance around the circle.

To find the circumference, use either formula below.

$C = \pi \times$ diameter or $C = \pi \times 2 \times$ radius

Find the circumference of this circle. Use 3.14 for π.

Circumference $= \pi \times$ diameter
Circumference $\approx 3.14 \times 5$ m
Circumference ≈ 15.7 m

Find the circumference of each circle. Use $\frac{22}{7}$ for π.

1.

14 in.

2.

$3\frac{1}{2}$ ft

3.

21 m

Find the circumference of each circle. Use 3.14 for π.

4. diameter = 5 cm   **5.** radius = 8 m   **6.** radius = 5 in.

7. diameter = 20 yd   **8.** diameter = 6.5 m   **9.** radius = .3 cm

CRITICAL THINKING

Solve each problem. Show your work.

1. The diameter of the reservoir is 800 yards. How many yards of fencing is needed to surround the reservoir? Would you use 3.14 or $\frac{22}{7}$ for π? Why?

2. A circling sprinkler sprays water with a radius of 14 feet. How much fencing is needed to surround the circle of wet grass? Would you use 3.14 or $\frac{22}{7}$ for π? Why?

▶ 16.11 Area of Circles   Exercise 152

To find the area of a circle, use this formula: Area = π × (radius.)^2.

Remember that to square the radius, you multiply the radius by itself.

Find the area of this circle. Use 3.14 for π.

Area = π × (radius)^2
Area ≈ 3.14 × 6 in. × 6 in.
Area ≈ 113.04 sq in.

12 in.

Find the area of each circle. Use 3.14 for π.

1.

1 in.

2.

3 cm

3.

9 ft

4. diameter = 20 in.   **5.** radius = 7 m   **6.** radius = 8 mm

7. diameter = 15 ft   **8.** radius = 5 in.   **9.** diameter = 25 yd

CRITICAL THINKING

Solve each problem. Show your work.

1. A sprinkler sprays water over a circle with a radius of 15 meters.
How large an area can the sprinkler water?

2. A circular carpet has a diameter of 6 feet. What is the area
of the carpet in square feet? What is the area in square yards?

▶ 16.12 Problem Solving: **Exercise 153**
   ## Subtracting to Find Area

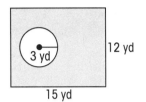

A drawing of a park is on the right. Grass grows
all around the pond in the park. What is the
area of the grassy part? Round the answer to
the nearest square yard.

PLAN
Find the area of the park.
Find the area of the pond.
Then subtract the areas.

DO
Area = 15 yd × 12 yd = 180 sq yd
Area ≈ 3.14 × 3 yd × 3 yd ≈ 28.26 sq yd
180 sq yd − 28.26 sq yd = 151.74 sq yd

The area of the grassy part is about 152 square yards.

**READ the problem. Draw a diagram. Make a PLAN to solve the problem.
Use 3.14 for π.**

1. The pool and deck area measures 75 ft by 100 ft.
   The pool is a rectangle that measures 50 ft by 80 ft.
   What is the area of the deck alone?

2. A circular picture with a radius of 1 in. is framed in a
   rectangular mat that is 4 in. by 6 in. What is the area
   of the mat without the picture?

3. A room that is 13 ft by 13 ft has a rug that measures
   9 ft by 6 ft. What is the area of the room that is not
   covered by the rug?

4. A triangular park area is covered with grass except
   for a monument with a circular base. The base of
   the monument has a radius of 2 ft. The base of the
   triangle is 5 ft. The height is 12 ft. What is the area
   of the part of the triangle covered with grass?

▶ 16.13 Volume of Prisms   Exercise 154

To find the volume of a rectangular prism or a cube, use this formula:

Volume = length × width × height

Find the volume of this prism.

Volume = length × width × height
Volume = 10 in. × 3 in. × 5 in.
Volume = 150 cu in.

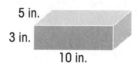

Find the volume of each prism.

1.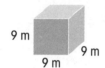
9 m
9 m
9 m

2. 7.5 ft
1 ft
1 ft

3.
.2 cm
.2 cm
.2 cm

4.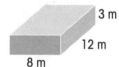
3 m
12 m
8 m

5.
5 in.
2.5 in.
2.5 in.

6. 12 yd
12 yd
12 yd

CRITICAL THINKING

Solve the problem. Show your work.

A gardener has a large rectangular planter that measures 12 ft by 2 ft by 3 ft. Each bag of potting soil will fill 2 cubic feet. How many bags does the gardener need to fill the planter?

▶ 16.14 Volume of Cylinders   **Exercise 155**

> To find the volume of a cylinder, use this formula:
>
> Volume = π × (radius)^2 × height
>
> Find the volume of this cylinder.
>
> Volume = π × (radius)^2 × height
> Volume ≈ 3.14 × 3 m × 3 m × 7 m
> Volume ≈ 197.82 cu m

Find the volume of each cylinder. Use 3.14 for π.

1.

2.

3.

4.

5.

6.

CRITICAL THINKING

Solve the problem. Show your work.

Find the volume of this shed. It is in
the shape of a prism and half a cylinder.

Name _____ Date _____

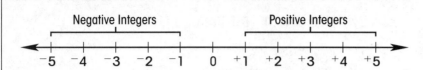

The numbers $^+5$ and $^-5$ are opposites. Opposites are the same distance from zero on the number line but are on opposite sides of zero.

Write the missing integers on the number line.

1.
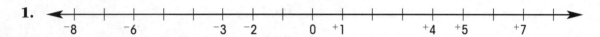

Write the opposite of each integer.

2. $^+2$ _____   **3.** $^-5$ _____   **4.** $^-7$ _____   **5.** $^+4$ _____

6. $^-1$ _____   **7.** $^-8$ _____   **8.** $^+3$ _____   **9.** $^-4$ _____

Write an integer to describe each situation.

10. Saundra gained 5 points in a game. _____   **11.** Ed lost $7 at the mall. _____

12. The diver was 19 feet below sea level. _____   **13.** The temperature rose 15°. _____

14. Nancy saved $5 from her allowance. _____   **15.** The temperature went down 34°. _____

16. The football player lost 7 yards. _____   **17.** The rocket rose 54 feet. _____

CRITICAL THINKING

Write an integer for each problem.

1. The opposite of the opposite of $^+5$.   **2.** The opposite of the opposite of $^-6$.

▶ 17.2 Adding Integers with Like Signs   Exercise 157

You can use number lines to add integers. Make the number line any size you need.

Start at zero. Move to the right to add positive integers.

Add. $^+4 + {}^+5$

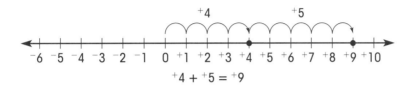

$^+4 + {}^+5 = {}^+9$

Start at zero. Move to the left to add negative integers.

Add. $^-3 + {}^-4$

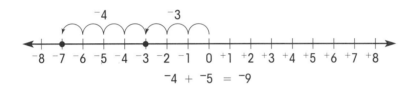

$^-4 + {}^-5 = {}^-9$

Add.

1. $^-3 + {}^-5 =$ **2.** $^+5 + {}^+6 =$ **3.** $^+8 + {}^+6 =$ **4.** $^-5 + {}^-9 =$

5. $^+3 + {}^+7 =$ **6.** $^+7 + {}^+5 =$ **7.** $^-7 + {}^-9 =$ **8.** $^-2 + {}^-5 =$

9. $^-7 + {}^-8 =$ **10.** $^-1 + {}^-6 =$ **11.** $^+9 + {}^+8 =$ **12.** $^-7 + {}^-4 =$

13. $^+9 + {}^+12 =$ **14.** $^-5 + {}^-8 =$ **15.** $^+11 + {}^+5 =$ **16.** $^+13 + {}^+7 =$

17. $^-12 + {}^-5 =$ **18.** $^+5 + {}^+9 =$ **19.** $^-6 + {}^-8 =$ **20.** $^+5 + {}^+8 =$

CRITICAL THINKING

The lowest temperature in Minnesota is $^-39°$F. The lowest temperature in Montana is 3°F lower than $^-39°$F. What is the lowest temperature in Montana?

▶ 17.3 Adding Integers with Unlike Signs   Exercise 158

You can add integers with unlike signs on a number line.

Add. $^-5 + {}^+7$

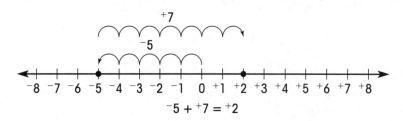

$$^-5 + {}^+7 = {}^+2$$

Add.

1. $^+5 + {}^-8 =$ **2.** $^-8 + {}^+10 =$ **3.** $^-8 + {}^+3 =$ **4.** $^-6 + {}^+4 =$

5. $^-7 + {}^+3 =$ **6.** $^+9 + {}^-7 =$ **7.** $^+2 + {}^-9 =$ **8.** $^+6 + {}^-12 =$

9. $^-4 + {}^+2 =$ **10.** $^-3 + {}^+10 =$ **11.** $^+9 + {}^-5 =$ **12.** $^+7 + {}^-8 =$

13. $^+4 + {}^-6 =$ **14.** $^-6 + {}^+13 =$ **15.** $^-10 + {}^+12 =$ **16.** $^+7 + {}^-4 =$

17. $^-5 + {}^+14 =$ **18.** $^+2 + {}^-5 =$ **19.** $^+16 + {}^-13 =$ **20.** $^-13 + {}^+4 =$

CRITICAL THINKING

Laura made $15 baby-sitting. She then spent $5 at school.
John gave Laura the $2 he owed her. Laura then spent $3 on
a new notebook. How much money does Laura have left?

Name _____ Date _____

To subtract an integer, add its opposite.

Subtract. $^-6 - {^+2}$

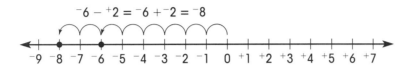

$$^-6 - {^+2} = {^-6} + {^-2} = {^-8}$$

Rewrite each subtraction problem as an addition problem. Do not solve.

1. $^+5 - {^+3}$ **2.** $^-4 - {^+6}$ **3.** $^+2 - {^+8}$ **4.** $^-9 - {^+5}$

5. $^-7 - {^+16}$ **6.** $^+8 - {^+12}$ **7.** $^-13 - {^+8}$ **8.** $^-8 - {^+3}$

Subtract. Remember to rewrite each problem as an addition problem.

9. $^+2 - {^+6} =$ **10.** $^+5 - {^+9} =$ **11.** $^+12 - {^-18} =$ **12.** $^-5 - {^+14} =$

13. $^-2 - {^-10} =$ **14.** $^-14 - {^-3} =$ **15.** $^+12 - {^+17} =$ **16.** $^-4 - {^+12} =$

17. $^-8 - {^-2} =$ **18.** $^+18 - {^+23} =$ **19.** $^-9 - {^-8} =$ **20.** $^-12 - {^+10} =$

CRITICAL THINKING

The highest temperature in Anchorage, Alaska for January is 20°F.
The highest temperature in Barrow, Alaska for January is $^-9$°F.

1. Which city has the colder temperature in January?

2. What is the difference between these temperatures?

17.5 Multiplying Integers   Exercise 160

When you multiply integers, you must decide if the answer is positive or negative.

If the signs of the integers are the **same**, the product is **positive**.	$^+5 \times {}^+4 = {}^+20$ $^-5 \times {}^-4 = {}^+20$
If the signs of the integers are **different**, the product is **negative**.	$^+5 \times {}^-4 = {}^-20$ $^-5 \times {}^+4 = {}^-20$

Multiply. Decide if the product is positive or negative.

1. $^-8 \times {}^+7 =$ 2. $^-3 \times {}^+12 =$ 3. $^+6 \times {}^-5 =$ 4. $^+3 \times {}^-10 =$

5. $^+4 \times {}^-9 =$ 6. $^+10 \times {}^-5 =$ 7. $^-8 \times {}^+6 =$ 8. $^+7 \times {}^-5 =$

9. $^-9 \times {}^-6 =$ 10. $^-8 \times {}^-9 =$ 11. $^+3 \times {}^+6 =$ 12. $^+5 \times {}^+8 =$

13. $^-4 \times {}^-8 =$ 14. $^+7 \times {}^+3 =$ 15. $^-6 \times {}^-2 =$ 16. $^-8 \times {}^-2 =$

17. $^-2 \times {}^+5 =$ 18. $^+7 \times {}^-5 =$ 19. $^-3 \times {}^+4 =$ 20. $^+6 \times {}^-4 =$

CRITICAL THINKING

1. Every day Jon saves $4 by bringing lunch to school. How much does Jon save after five days of school? Is this a positive or a negative number? Why?

2. Every day Aaron buys a school lunch that costs $4.50. How much does he spend altogether for five days of lunches? Is this a negative or a positive number? Why?

▶ 17.6 Dividing Integers   Exercise 161

The rules for dividing integers are the same as the rules for multiplying integers.

If the signs of the integers are the **same**, $^-36 \div {}^-9 = +4$
the quotient is **positive**. $^+36 \div +9 = {}^+4$

If the signs of the integers are **different**, $^-36 \div {}^+9 = {}^-4$
the quotient is **negative**. $^+36 \div {}^-9 = {}^-4$

Divide. Decide if the sign of the quotient is positive or negative.

1. $^-8 \div {}^+4 =$ **2.** $^+5 \div {}^-5 =$ **3.** $^+16 \div {}^-8 =$ **4.** $^+24 \div {}^-4 =$

5. $^-56 \div {}^+7 =$ **6.** $^+18 \div {}^-6 =$ **7.** $^-15 \div {}^+5 =$ **8.** $^-10 \div {}^+2 =$

9. $^-9 \div {}^-3 =$ **10.** $^+21 \div {}^+7 =$ **11.** $^+28 \div {}^+4 -$ **12.** $^-24 \div {}^-6 =$

13. $^-32 \div {}^-4 =$ **14.** $^+48 \div {}^+6 =$ **15.** $^-45 \div {}^-9 =$ **16.** $^-54 \div {}^-9 =$

17. $^+12 \div {}^-6 =$ **18.** $^+56 \div {}^-8 =$ **19.** $^-63 \div {}^+9 =$ **20.** $^-72 \div {}^+8 =$

21. $^+18 \div {}^+9 =$ **22.** $^-15 \div {}^-5 =$ **23.** $^-21 \div {}^+3 =$ **24.** $^+27 \div {}^+9 =$

CRITICAL THINKING

Find the missing integer for each problem.

1. $^+18 \div$ ____ $= {}^-9$ **2.** ____ $\div {}^-5 = {}^+6$ **3.** $^-24 \div$ ____ $= {}^+2$ **4.** $^+18 \div$ ____ $= {}^+3$

▶ 17.7 Problem Solving: Using Integers   Exercise 162

The surface of Lake Superior is about 183 meters above sea level. It is about 406 meters deep at its deepest point. How many meters below sea level is the deepest point?

PLAN   Lake surface   + 183 meters
          Depth of lake   − 406 meters
          Add to find meters below sea level.

DO   Add.
          $^+183$ m + $^-406$ m = $^-223$ m

Lake Superior's deepest point is 233 meters below sea level.

READ the problem. Make a PLAN. DO the plan to solve the problem.

1. Steven scored a total of 140 points in seven basketball games. What was his average score?

2. The Wildcats football team lost 5 yards in each of three plays. What was the team's total loss?

3. A kite was flying at a height of 97 meters. The wind lowered the height by 5 meters. What is the new height of the kite?

4. In Spearfish, South Dakota the temperature was 20°F. It got 27°F colder that day. What was the temperature after the change?

5. The lowest point in the United States is about 86 meters below sea level ($^-86$ m). The highest point is about 6,193 meters above sea level ($^+6,193$ m). What is the difference between these points?

18.1 What Is an Equation?   **Exercise 163**

To solve an equation, find the value of the variable that makes the equation true.

Is $b = 3$ the solution to the equation?	$4b = 12$
Replace b with 3 in the equation.	$4 \times 3?\ 12$
	$12 = 12$ ✓

Yes, $b = 3$ is the solution to the equation.

Tell whether the number is a solution to the equation. Write *Yes* or *No*.

1. $c + 5 = 14;\ c = 8$ **2.** $k + 8 = 18;\ k = 7$ **3.** $x - 8 = 23;\ x = 31$

4. $h - 16 = 20;\ h = 36$ **5.** $n + 11 = 25;\ n = 12$ **6.** $a + 7 = 17;\ a = 11$

7. $x - 8 = 23;\ x = 15$ **8.** $n - 4 = 19;\ n = 23$ **9.** $v + 7 = 15;\ v = 22$

10. $n + 3 = 22;\ n = 19$ **11.** $3x = 21;\ x = 8$ **12.** $4w = 36;\ w = 9$

13. $7a = 42;\ a = 7$ **14.** $z \div 5 = 9;\ z = 45$ **15.** $c \div 7 = 7;\ c = 1$

16. $14 \div h = 2;\ h = 7$ **17.** $27 \div k = 9;\ k = 3$ **18.** $7 \div w = 7;\ w = 1$

CRITICAL THINKING

Choose the equation that fits the situation described below.

A panda arrived at the zoo in a cage that weighed 28 kilograms. The total weight of the cage and the panda was 139 kilograms. What was the weight of the panda?

a. $139 + x = 28$ **b.** $139 + 28 = x$ **c.** $x + 28 = 139$

▶ 18.2 Using Parentheses   Exercise 164

> Parentheses around an operation tell you to do this operation first.
>
> Simplify. $(8 + 2) - 5 =$ $3(12 - 7) + 4 =$
> $10 \quad - 5 = 5$ $3(5) \quad + 4 =$
> $15 \quad + 4 = 19$

Simplify each expression. Remember to do what is in the parentheses first.

1. $(9 - 5) + 7$ **2.** $5 + 9(2 + 4)$ **3.** $19 - (5 + 7)$

4. $(5 + 8) + (6 - 2)$ **5.** $95 - (50 - 7)$ **6.** $(52 - 26) + 24$

7. $(3 \times 9) + (4 \times 8)$ **8.** $(12 \times 5) - (8 \times 7)$ **9.** $(23 + 4) \div 9$

10. $5(5 + 8) - (2 \times 8)$ **11.** $(9 \times 5) + 3(5 \times 4)$ **12.** $5(7 \times 8) - (8 - 4)$

13. $7 + (38 - 5)$ **14.** $39 - 2(3 + 8)$ **15.** $3(8 + 5) + 2(7 - 2)$

CRITICAL THINKING

Simplify each expression.

1. a. $19 + (8 + 7)$ **b.** $(19 + 8) + 7$

2. a. $19 - (8 - 7)$ **b.** $(19 - 8) - 7$

3. a. $(12 \times 4) \times 2$ **b.** $12 \times (4 \times 2)$

4. a. $(12 \div 4) \div 2$ **b.** $12 \div (4 \div 2)$

▶ 18.3 Order of Operations

Simplify.	$29 - 5 \times 4$
Do all the multiplication and division first from left to right. Then do all addition and subtraction from left to right.	$29 - 20$
	9
The value of $29 - 5 \times 4$ is 9.	

Simplify each expression. Remember to multiply or divide first.

1. $53 + 12 \times 10$ **2.** $16 + 93 - 18$ **3.** $42 - 5 \times 2$

4. $48 + 12 \times 3$ **5.** $88 \div 8 \times 7$ **6.** $33 + 5 \times 8$

7. $12 + 72 \div 8$ **8.** $67 - 23 + 39$ **9.** $4 \times 5 + 27$

10. $27 \div 3 \times 4$ **11.** $53 - 12 \times 3$ **12.** $28 + 12 \times 20$

13. $19 \times 8 - 4$ **14.** $12 \times 3 + 21$ **15.** $9 \times 11 - 8 \times 8$

CRITICAL THINKING

Candy is shopping for four dresses for a new job. Each dress costs the same. The four dresses she wants cost $192 altogether.

1. How much does one dress cost? Use the expression $192 \div 4$ to find the cost of one dress.

2. How much do three dresses cost? Use the expression $192 \div 4 \times 3$, to find the cost of three dresses.

3. Is the expression $192 \div 4 \times 3$ equivalent to $192 \div (4 \times 3)$? Why or why not?

Name _____ Date _____

▶ 18.4 Solving Equations with Addition and Subtraction Exercise 166

To solve equations with addition or subtraction, **undo** each operation.

Solve.

$x + 7 = 15$		$x - 5 = 13$
$x + 7 - 7 = 15 - 7$	Undo the addition or subtraction.	$x - 5 + 5 = 13 + 5$
$x + 0 = 8$	Simplify each side.	$x + 0 = 18$
$x = 8$		$x = 18$
$8 + 7 \; ? \; 15$	Check the solution.	$18 - 5 \; ? \; 13$
$15 = 15 \checkmark$		$13 = 13 \checkmark$

Solve each equation. Check your work.

1. $y + 5 = 12$ **2.** $r - 14 = 20$ **3.** $d + 9 = 14$

4. $s - 56 = 23$ **5.** $t + 58 = 78$ **6.** $w - 45 = 32$

7. $q + 4 = 11$ **8.** $t - 4 = 8$ **9.** $m + 7 = 20$

10. $76 = x + 42$ **11.** $14 = r - 5$ **12.** $10 = s - 25$

CRITICAL THINKING

Solve each problem. Show your work.

1. Tina is 4 years older than John. If Tina is 12 years old, how old is John?

2. Tina is 25 years younger than her mother. If Tina is 12 years old, how old is her mother?

166   Chapter 18 • Algebra

Copyright © by Globe Fearon, Inc. All rights reserved.

▶ 18.5 Solving Equations with Multiplication and Division

To solve equations with multiplication or division, *undo* each operation.

Solve.

$5b = 15$ $\dfrac{m}{5} = 4$

$\dfrac{5b}{5} = \dfrac{15}{5}$ Undo the multiplication $\dfrac{m}{5} \times 5 = 4 \times 5$
                                                  or division.

$b = 3$ Simplify each side. $m = 20$

$5\,(3)\ ?\ 15$ Check the solution. $\dfrac{20}{5}\ ?\ 4$
$15 = 15\ \checkmark$ $4 = 4\ \checkmark$

Solve each equation. Check your work.

1. $3a = 15$ **2.** $9n = 81$ **3.** $10c = 100$

4. $\dfrac{s}{6} = 6$ **5.** $\dfrac{k}{9} = 45$ **6.** $\dfrac{r}{4} = 20$

7. $8n = 64$ **8.** $100 = 25m$ **9.** $\dfrac{c}{9} = 63$

10. $49 = \dfrac{n}{7}$ **11.** $7u = 77$ **12.** $8r = 96$

CRITICAL THINKING

Solve each problem. Show your work.

1. Bridget is twice as old as Joan.
     If Bridget is 20 years old, how old is Joan?

2. Bridget's age is $\dfrac{1}{4}$ of her grandmother's age.
     If Bridget is 20 years old, how old is her grandmother?

▶ 18.6 Problem Solving: Exercise 168
Using a One-Step Equation

You can use $d = r \times t$ to solve distance problems.

The Smiths drove 220 miles at an average speed of 55 miles per hour. How long did the trip take?

PLAN   Substitute the values you know into the equation $d = r \times t$. Then, solve.

DO $220 = 55\,t$

$$\frac{220}{55} = \frac{55}{55}t$$

$$4 \;=\; t$$

The trip took 4 hours.

READ the problem. Make a PLAN. DO the plan to solve the problem.

1. A train went 450 miles at 75 miles per hour. How long did the trip take?

2. A plane went 1,575 miles in 5 hours. What was the plane's average rate in miles per hour?

3. Jose drove for 5 hours at a rate of 52 mile per hour. How far did he travel?

4. Rachel drove for 4 hours at a rate of 47 miles per hour. How far did she travel?

5. A plane flew for 6 hours. It went 320 miles per hour. How far did it go?

6. Tara walked for 2 hours at a rate of 1 mile every 20 minutes. How many miles did she walk in 1 hour? (Remember that 60 minutes = 1 hour.) How many miles did she walk altogether?

▶ 18.7 Solving Equations with More Than One Operation

To solve equations with more than one operation, undo the addition or the subtraction first, and then undo the multiplication or the division.

Solve for *a*.

$$5a - 7 = 28$$

First, undo the addition or subtraction.

$$5a - 7 + 7 = 28 + 7$$

$$5a = 35$$

$$\frac{a}{6} + 2 = 6$$

$$\frac{a}{6} + 2 - 2 = 6 - 2$$

$$\frac{a}{6} = 4$$

$$\frac{5a}{5} = \frac{35}{5}$$

$$a = 7$$

Then, undo the multiplication or division.

$$6 \times \frac{a}{6} = 4 \times 6$$

$$a = 24$$

$$5(7) - 7 \text{ ? } 28$$

Check the solution.

$$35 - 7 \text{ ? } 28$$

$$28 = 28 \checkmark$$

$$\frac{24}{6} + 2 \text{ ? } 6$$

$$4 + 2 \text{ ? } 6$$

$$6 = 6 \checkmark$$

Solve each equation.

1. $2y - 9 = 1$

2. $4x + 5 = 45$

3. $3m - 2 = 16$

4. $3a + 5 = 38$

5. $2y - 8 = 12$

6. $4x - 8 = 0$

7. $5u - 12 = 18$

8. $\frac{n}{5} + 4 = 21$

9. $\frac{a}{6} + 7 = 35$

10. $\frac{x}{9} - 9 = 81$

11. $\frac{y}{10} - 10 = 100$

12. $\frac{w}{8} + 6 = 74$

CRITICAL THINKING

Use the equation $F = 1.8C + 32$ to answer each question below.

1. What is 100° Celsius (*C*) equal to in degrees Fahrenheit (*F*)?

2. What is 32° Fahrenheit (*F*) equal to in degrees Celsius (*C*)?

▶ 18.8 Problem Solving: Using a Two-Step Equation

You can use $c = r \times d + f$ to solve rental problems.

The cost to rent a pair of skis is $8 a day plus a renter's fee of $10. Howard paid $34 to rent a pair of skis. For how many days will he be renting the skis?

PLAN Substitute the values you know into the equation $c = r \times d + f$. Then solve.

DO
$$34 = 8d + 10$$
$$34 - 10 = 8d + 10 - 10$$
$$24 = 8d$$
$$\frac{24}{8} = \frac{8d}{8}$$
$$3 = d$$

Howard will rent skis for 3 days.

READ the problem. Make a PLAN. DO the plan to solve the problem.

1. The cost to rent a tent is $14 per day plus a fee of $45. Mrs. Donnely rented a tent for $101. For how many days did she rent the tent?

2. The cost to rent a table is $6 per day plus a fee of $18. The Photography Club paid a total of $30 to rent a table. For how many days did it rent the table?

3. The cost to rent a car is $69 per day plus a fee of $15. Mr. Bradley rented a car for $429. For how many days did he rent the car?

4. The cost to rent a pool table is $20 per day plus a fee of $5. The After-School Club paid $85 for the table. For how many days did the club rent the table?